# LANGUAGE

MW00810810

Dorothy S
Celia Genishi and
ADVISORY BOARD: *Richard Alli*
*Anne Haas Dyson, Carole Edelsky, M*

*continued*

For volumes in the NCRLL Collection (edited by JoBeth Allen and Donna E. Alvermann) and the Practitioners Bookshelf Series
(edited by Celia Genishi and Donna E. Alvermann), as well as other titles in this series, please visit www.tcpress.com.

# SOCIAL JUSTICE LITERACIES IN THE ENGLISH CLASSROOM

*Teaching Practice in Action*

ASHLEY S. BOYD

FOREWORD BY DEBORAH APPLEMAN

**TEACHERS COLLEGE PRESS**

**TEACHERS COLLEGE** | COLUMBIA UNIVERSITY

NEW YORK AND LONDON

Published by Teachers College Press, 1234 Amsterdam Avenue, New York, NY 10027

Copyright © 2017 by Teachers College, Columbia University

All rights reserved. No part of this publication may be reproduced or transmitted in any form or by any means, electronic or mechanical, including photocopy, or any information storage and retrieval system, without permission from the publisher. For reprint permission and other subsidiary rights requests, please contact Teachers College Press, Rights Dept.: tcpressrights@tc.columbia.edu

*Library of Congress Cataloging-in-Publication Data is available at loc.gov*

ISBN 978-0-8077-5826-7 (paper)
ISBN 978-0-8077-5863-2 (hardcover)
ISBN 978-0-8077-7662-9 (ebook)

Printed on acid-free paper
Manufactured in the United States of America

24  23  22  21  20  19  18  17        8  7  6  5  4  3  2  1

*For my mom, who instilled in me an unwavering belief in the power of education, and for the three teachers within these pages who welcomed me into their classrooms and into their hearts. Your tireless efforts for your students do not go unnoticed.*

# Contents

**PART III: SOCIAL JUSTICE BEYOND THE WALLS
OF THE ENGLISH CLASSROOM**

# Foreword

What does it mean to teach English? What is the purpose of language arts classes or, more broadly, literacy instruction—especially in the 21st century, which is gifted with technological advances but hamstrung by seemingly impossible issues of inequity and social injustice? For Ashley Boyd and the three dedicated English teachers that she profiles in this volume, the answer is that we teach language arts to make a better world for our students and to help them make a better world for themselves. Furthermore, Boyd convincingly argues, we do that by incorporating a social justice approach to literacy in our English classrooms.

In the many decades and even centuries since English teaching began, the responses to what English classrooms should emphasize has radically changed. We have moved from a cultural transmission model of literary treasures to a skills model that teaches the basics of reading and writing, and now to a standards-driven model like the Common Core, where ubiquitous standardized tests seem to drive our instruction. Of course, these approaches are not discrete; they intermingle imperfectly and with varied results in our practice. They each also have their own strengths and limitations, supporters and detractors, and their own political, pedagogical, and ideological baggage.

In the last decade or so, the concept of teaching through the lens of social justice has gained traction in a variety of teaching disciplines—science, social studies, even math. Originally grown from critical pedagogical perspectives—including feminist pedagogies, multicultural education pedagogies, and critical race theory—the notion of teaching for social justice holds great promise for educators across the K–college spectrum. This is especially relevant in language arts classrooms, where the critical study of texts in social context and language and power can help students learn to connect their lived realities to the worlds of the text.

Perhaps it is commonplace these days to quote the inimitable educator and philosopher Paulo Freire, but his charge to help students "learn to read both the word and the world" is to me the bedrock responsibility of English teaching; it has certainly guided my own work in helping students learn to read and if necessary resist ideology for literary theory. Social justice approaches to English classrooms, however, have their detractors. There are those who think it is a kind of ideological brainwashing or proselytizing. Others worry that the social justice agenda can eclipse the important transmission of skills. Still others may simplify the project by simply focusing on a more inclusive text selection. While diverse literary perspectives are important, the author rightfully points out that social justice classrooms include other important elements, as well as teachers and students working together to, as she puts it, "name oppression and work critically toward social justice."

Above everything else, I think that a common ground for English teachers has been that we want our classrooms to be humane. We want students to see themselves reflected not only in what we teach, but in how we teach. We want our language arts classes to be places where students can ask questions that really matter to them, such as questions about equity and social justice. Although it may sound mawkish or overly sentimental, we need to admit to ourselves that not only do we want students to become better readers and better writers, but also that we want them to become better people.

At the end of this book (spoiler alert!), Ashley Boyd shares the following vision of a field of English education that embraces social justice literacies:

> I reenvision ours as a space thriving with lively conversation based on reading, dissecting, and reconstructing texts that center current events and local concerns. I imagine students engaged with social action projects, tackling issues of import to them in their immediate as well as broader contexts. I foresee the selection of new texts in classrooms, those that reflect the positions of our students and that challenge them to think and see beyond themselves. I picture students who come to value one another's differences and seek out diverse perspectives.

This is an appealing vision for the future, for it bears much promise— for our classrooms, and also for the future our students will both shape and inhabit.

—*Deborah Appleman*

# Preface

I entered my career as a high school English teacher years ago in a rural area and was ready to enact critical teaching and to change the world. My preparation program was one committed to equity and had instilled in me a commitment to honoring student diversity and to teaching students how to question and reconstruct their worlds. Although my foundation was strong, I quickly realized that my goals often conflicted with those of the system in which I worked and that the institution of schooling was much more complicated than I initially grasped. Testing, maintaining the status quo, working with colleagues of varied positions and discipline areas, and balancing the responsibilities of teaching, coaching, and counseling were at times overwhelming. Nonetheless, I found that reminding myself of the values that led me to the profession provided small moments of success and allowed for my own growth as an educator as well as for the development of my students' understanding and dispositions. And still, I wanted more—more knowledge, more theory, and more practice with the sort of teaching I envisioned, to provide an education that captivated students and engaged them with social injustices so that they could act on them. I returned to graduate school to seek additional learning opportunities and to work with preservice and inservice teachers toward learning those methods for critical teaching.

As I transitioned to my role as a teacher educator, I worked diligently to instill in my preservice teacher candidates a passion for social justice. We read about culturally responsive teaching, antiracist pedagogy, and multicultural education. Yet despite their understandings of these theoretical viewpoints, they consistently asked me, "But how do I do this . . . *in English*?" What they sought were authentic examples of teachers doing the work, of translating theory into discipline-specific practice. Prompted by their inquiries, I undertook years of research, much of which was spent in the classrooms of the teachers in this book, to respond adequately to my teacher candidates' inquiries. I completed months of observations in middle and high school classrooms, collecting lesson plans, assignments, and school documents, and interviewing teachers and students, querying their conceptions and implementations of social justice.

What I learned from my own experiences with teaching and from the time I have spent researching is that there are myriad ways to do social justice, to work for equity and change with students. What I share here, which I now also share with my teacher candidates, are those models of secondary English teachers who are committed to equity and criticality at every turn in their professions. Doing this work is not easy; there are setbacks and challenges. Teaching strategies that position students as critical consumers of knowledge and introducing approaches that incite them to action will meet controversy. From these teachers' work, however, I have also identified ways to overcome and circumvent those potential conflicts.

I hope to provide then, for both teacher candidates and inservice teachers, compelling arguments for the necessity of teaching for social justice. I also intend to show the various possibilities for embracing critical teaching through analyzing portraits of educators who have harnessed their backgrounds and dispositions to work for a more equitable society and to envision an English education in which analysis and action are central. The urgency of approaching curriculum in this way cannot be overstated—it not only creates a more relevant and engaging classroom but it facilitates students' growth as discerning individuals who can analytically engage with numerous topics through assorted mediums. No longer can we treat ours as a static discipline, giving attention only to texts written years ago, examining their literary worth at the exclusion of considering what is happening in society today. Our world is changing rapidly, and social, political, and environmental concerns affect every element of our daily lives. We must invite that world into our classrooms so that our students can understand, debate, and address it in innovative, thoughtful ways. It is thus our job, as English educators, to involve our students with texts that are both personal and political and to interact with those texts and contexts so as to make the world more inclusive and just. The examples in this book illustrate specific ways to accomplish this task.

## ACKNOWLEDGMENTS

There are so many people who made possible the writing here. First, I must thank the three teachers who allowed me into their classrooms daily for the research that led to this book. The real Etta, Beverly, and Tate are remarkable individuals. I am eternally grateful for your trust and friendship. To my UNC family: George Noblit, you taught me how to teach social justice with love and care, and you have proven that a teacher's role extends well beyond the time a student is in his class; Jim Trier, you taught me how to be an English educator and what being critical *really* means; Julie Justice, you showed me how to conduct research with attention to detail and inspired me to think more deeply about the topics of my work; Jocelyn Glazier, you believed in me, pushed me to produce material of which I am proud, challenged me, and showed me what it means to be an academic *and* a teacher

*and* a person. There really are not enough words to describe how much I
grew while under your guidance. Thank you to Lynda Stone for your years
of work with teacher candidates, myself included, and for teaching all of
us to "survive and subvert," to find creative ways to work in schools for
democracy and justice. I thank you all for molding me into the scholar I am
today.

To my critical friends: Rachel Harrington Surles, Michaela Birdyshaw,
Liz Dorris, Alison LaGarry, Katy Malley, Jeanne Dyches, Mandy Bean,
Summer Pennell, Hillary Parkhouse, Esmeralda Rodríguez, Tim Conder,
Janine Darragh, Johnna Lash, Brooklyn Walter, Anne Marie Guerrettaz,
Matthew Jeffries, Nicole Ferry, Shannon Gleason, and Kaylan Petrie—I am
so thankful for your camaraderie, support, and love. Without you to laugh
with and cry to, this book never would have come to fruition.

I have had the privilege of teaching many wonderful students in my
career thus far—fascinating individuals who have taught me as much as I
could ever have taught them. Although I cannot thank each one (but wish
I could), I would like to express my gratitude to Erica Adkins, Mary Ann
Kincer, Holly Matteson, Sydney Robertson, Alyssa Bauermeister, Taylor Be-
reiter, and Ruben Zecena for contributing to my learning of critical teaching
and my understandings of social justice.

To my colleagues at WSU who welcomed me with open arms and
buoyed my efforts in writing, I offer my gratitude. Patty Ericcson, Beth Buy-
serie, and Nancy Bell were instrumental in helping me find my way in our
department and guiding me when I needed it most. Bill Condon was the
best, most patient mentor as I navigated my way through book contracts
and annual reviews; Todd Butler has been an incredibly supportive chair,
offering advice, direction, and basketball metaphors; Roger Whitson and
Leeann Hunter have been not only friends but also co-pilots as I chartered
the new waters of academia. Victor Villaneuva was influential in helping me
get this work off the ground, reading early proposal drafts and providing
feedback. And Brenda Barrio has never left an email unanswered and has
always offered insight. I am thankful for each of you. I also want to thank
Melanie Shoffner and Jeffrey Reaser for their assistance in traversing the
field and with decisionmaking with regard to aspects of this book. To Emily
Spangler and the folks at Teachers College Press, thank you for your astute
advice, suggestions, and feedback.

Finally, I offer my sincere thanks to my family. To my parents, Brian and
Ginger, and Michael and Christy—thank you for always grounding me and
lifting me up. My mom, who is forever my number one fan, has lived every
moment of this process with me, unwearyingly reminding me that I could
do it and to trust in myself. To my heart, my five nieces: Avery, Lillian, Ellis,
Wren, and Ember, thank you for your unconditional love and your passion
for life. To my Fulfs family, thank you for always asking about my progress
and for so generously welcoming me into your lives and homes. You all

have made such a difference for me, an East Coast girl so far from home. Especially to Cody, Casey, and Dallas, thank you for allowing me into your worlds. Finally, to Keith, thank you for your eternal patience and love as I have worked into the night, for listening unceasingly as I hit roadblocks, for celebrating with me as I reached each benchmark, and for being an all-around wonderful human. I'm not sure how I got so lucky to have you in my life, but I am certain I am grateful.

## OVERVIEW OF BOOK

This book is divided into three parts. In Part I, I define social justice and argue for the need for social change, setting the stage for schools as sites for transformation. I then construct the relationships between social justice and English Language Arts, paying particular attention to the teacher's role as an equity agent. Sharing their backgrounds, dispositions, and teaching contexts, I present the three teachers whose practice I analyze in subsequent chapters to demonstrate how they exemplify real-life examples of social justice teaching.

Part II names and explores the social justice aspects of those three secondary English teachers who are working for equity in their classrooms. I first identify methods related primarily to pedagogies external to literary and informational texts and illustrate how building relationships with students and utilizing language in the classroom (Chapter 3) and caring for youth (Chapter 4) can be embodied specifically for the goals of justice. Through authentic scenarios, I assess how teachers advocate for students from minoritized populations and how they disrupt oppression through dialogue. In Chapter 5, I investigate the teachers' approaches that are purposely connected to content and explore how they select texts, locate resources, and work within district mandates to honor their critical dispositions. I also distinguish the methods that they use with traditional content, including the English canon, and how they employ multimodal texts to cultivate students' critical consciousness. At the end of each of these three chapters, I provide pedagogic advice for translating the methods outlined into teachers' practice.

In Part III, I build from the three teachers' practices to consider how educators can advance social justice endeavors through action projects and through providing a space for students to move on the injustices they see in their local, national, and global communities. I anticipate the challenges to social justice and action projects and provide suggestions for overcoming those obstacles, including establishing partnerships with colleagues, parents, and community members. Finally, I end with the possibilities I envision for the future of English education, hoping for more dynamic spaces that interrogate our social milieu.

# SOCIAL JUSTICE LITERACIES IN THE ENGLISH CLASSROOM

# Part I

# SOCIAL JUSTICE AND THE TEACHER

# CHAPTER 1

# Social Justice and English

I once asked a group of middle school students what they thought it meant when a teacher embodied "social justice." Upon hearing this question, an African American female student defined it as being "knowledgeable" and gave an example: Her mother raised her in an environment where "Black consciousness" was important and ensured that she knew about her ancestry. When this student approached her White female teacher with information on the narratives of Malcolm X and the history of protests by African Americans in her state, the teacher engaged in conversation with her about related authors and issues. Sometimes in class, according to the student, her teacher "reminded me of things my mom would say." The teacher also incorporated texts into her teaching that the student's mother had read with her at home. To this student, an educator's knowing about and engaging youth on topics like racism, oppression, and culture was evidence of social justice teaching.

Another White female student in the same conversation shared that she felt her teacher exhibited social justice in her role as the basketball coach. One of the student's peers had experienced a "rough time," and although not many people knew that she was facing abuse at home, their teacher "really helped her get through that" and adjust to a new living situation. To this student, social justice teaching involved caring, especially about people who are marginalized in some way. Taken together, these students' comments illustrate two of the components of the definition of social justice on which I rely. I believe *social justice* denotes a commitment to understanding, studying, and continuously discerning systems of oppression *and* to taking action to work against those structures for a better and more equitable society for all individuals.

Unfortunately, however, we live in a world where justice does not always exist, at least not for everyone, and where oppression is woven so intricately into the fabric of our society that many do not see it. Social justice therefore first means recognizing that systems of domination exist. These are entities such as sexism and heteronormativity, whereby not all members of society experience equity. While people sometimes think of these as individualized, discriminatory acts, such as assuming people will steal because of the color of their skin, I refer to them as systems because they combine to operate on a larger level, involving "pervasive, historical, political relationships of unequal power among social groups" (Sensoy & DiAngelo, 2012, p. 43). The emphasis on power is key—while anyone can hold a prejudice, when there is power within an interaction that is socially sanctioned it becomes a much larger problem. In addition, acts of oppression are often not seen as such because of the way they are presented, which poses an even greater conundrum for addressing them. For instance, the separation of bathrooms by gender is an age-old tradition in U.S. society, yet it privileges the gender binary, excluding those who do not subscribe to the distinction. Social justice involves exposing these sorts of systems, which are supported by tradition, and examining the authority that such customs maintain.

Second, once individuals understand that oppression exists, social justice involves assuming a critical disposition toward actions and systems that dominate society and individuals. This includes examining and approaching with a critical eye the parts of people's everyday lives—things such as media, conversations with friends, and interactions they see regularly—that they often take for granted. Once individuals assume this position, they question everything, wondering how a certain representation in a film might perpetuate a stereotype or how a news report has been constructed to tell the story a certain way. They even interrogate their own choices, such as whom they choose to sit beside in class or at the doctor's office or why they might prefer certain television shows over others, for how those decisions might have been influenced by social forces.

Finally, it is not enough to merely know that oppression exists and to query the world; individuals who believe in social equity must do something about injustice. They must act for social change when they recognize that what is happening in their society serves to privilege some while subjugating others. Social class divisions leave many people without adequate health care and education, causing them to struggle to live above the poverty line despite working several jobs. Racial profiling continues to cause the deaths of young African American men. There remains a significant gap in wage earnings between women and men. Homophobia and heteronormativity perpetuate bullying and validate gross acts of violence. These systems warrant change. As a society, we must address these shortcomings to create a more just existence for all. Even if it means that some will have to call their own privilege into question, certain individuals cannot continue to benefit from others' loss. Addressing systemic oppression is a moral obligation to make the world better and fair for *all* people. This could include being a social activist and participating in movements for a cause; disrupting normalized discriminatory language and using opportunities to expose others to how they propagate harmful stereotypes; or assuming a decisionmaking position on any scale, small or large, to direct policies in an organization.

Acting for social change also includes teaching, a profession that allows for preparing others to become those activists, concerned citizens, or policymakers. Teaching is itself a form of activism that allows for the realization of social justice both in *how* and *what* educators teach their students. Schools, as social spaces reflective of our diverse society and as places ripe with the potential to shape individuals' thinking and actions, are perfectly situated for effecting change. In the remainder of this book I examine how discerning oppression, questioning its myriad forms, and acting to address the institutions and structures that inhibit people and create inequity can translate into teachers' practice in schools. I investigate how teachers can embody their own social justice values in their teaching as well as how they can cultivate their students' critical stances and support the actions of youth to address injustices. I focus particularly on the field of English Language Arts in secondary schools, as this discipline affords vast opportunities for the enactment of social justice.

## SOCIAL JUSTICE IN ENGLISH LANGUAGE ARTS

Teachers have the capacity to integrate materials, guide conversations, and nurture their students' knowledge around a host of topics. While district mandates and required curriculum do exist and often feel limiting, teachers have the ability to make choices within parameters that greatly affect their students. English Language Arts (ELA) readily lends itself to social justice because it centers on texts for study, including print and media, and the content of those texts as well as how teachers work with them in the classroom can be embraced with critical goals in mind. In ELA, teachers and students examine how texts worked in the era in which they were created as well as how they are understood in their own milieu (Monroe, 2002). They analyze language in texts, examining meaning and positioning (Christensen, 2000); they dissect characters, exploring motive and development; and they discuss a range of themes from love and hate to adventure and darkness. Teachers draw connections to texts from students' lives and environments as well as from broader society. With students, they look for author's purpose, tone, and style. They read for universality, but they encourage their students to see the unique elements in a piece of literature.

These same text-based strategies can be employed from a social justice angle. When teachers and students look at context, they can ask questions about who was privileged in that era and how this fits in with their own. They can choose to look at historic events through texts that were pivotal in fights for justice, as there are both nonfiction and fiction documents readily available for such study. Students can examine not only the meanings of words, but how those meanings are attached to power and how they affirm or negate social positions (Delpit, 1995). When educators draw connections to students' lives, they can focus on validating their students' stories (Gay, 2002) *and* they can craft bridges to current local, national, and global events that are connected to social issues (Carey-Webb, 2001) and warrant student attention. From that attention, ELA teachers also have the opportunity to engage students in social action (Bomer & Bomer, 2001), a practice that involves literacy at every step, such as writing government officials, speaking at school or community events, and generating alternative and informative texts on issues. Social justice; thinking and talking about the world in ways that promote equity; and ELA, a space of myriad texts that reflect the world, are a perfect fit.

Yet there is a historic misunderstanding about social justice teaching and English. Some think that equity manifests in the field simply in the form of text selection, and that if students are exposed to works written by authors of diverse ethnicities, social classes, geographic areas, and sexual orientations, goals for fairness and exposure have been met. And truly, those goals might be, but social justice encompasses much more. Banks (2010) has famously called covering a diverse range of authors something akin to the "heroes and holidays" approach, wherein teachers include individuals of different backgrounds in curriculum in celebratory, yet superficial, ways and check off some sort of list for meeting a diversity requirement. Well-meaning teachers often strive to integrate different perspectives into their text choices, knowing that the viewpoints of authors of color, for instance, have been historically excluded from the canon.

While inclusive curriculum is important and is part of social justice, it does not fully meet the goals of equity-oriented practices. I could read, for example, *Their Eyes Were Watching God* (Hurston, 1937/1994) with a group of students, and I have included a female author of color. Yet to do this without exploring critical aspects, such as how language is connected to power or how modern-day racism exists, would leave unexamined aspects of social justice. There is thus a *critical* component that is vital and central to doing social justice in English. Merely exposing students to perspectives other their own without engaging them explicitly in topics of oppression, privilege, and power is not enough. There is much more than introducing content, although it is a place to start and is central to study, that occurs with social justice practice in English. Subject matter alone leaves uncharted elements of a social justice classroom, such as building relationships, using inclusive language practices, and cultivating societal critique, to name a few.

## SOCIAL JUSTICE LITERACIES: A THEORETICAL LENS

There is, however, not just one way to work for change through schools. In fact, there are a multitude of methods that English teachers might employ to demonstrate how they name oppression and work critically toward social justice in their classrooms with students. I, following Hines and Johnson (2007) and Johnson (2012) view the various avenues that teachers take as *social justice literacies*. Framing the work from this perspective allows for growth and flexibility in the ways teachers do social justice as well as where exactly and with whom they choose, as educators, to engage on this level.

The notion that pedagogies for social justice can be associated with literacy comes out of the work of scholars in the field of New Literacy Studies (NLS) who posited literacies as social practices (Barton & Hamilton, 1998), as actions that occur within a context. In my work here, the contexts are classrooms with teachers who work for social justice. While literacy is traditionally defined and referred to in public arenas as simply reading, writing, and skills that can be measured (Street, 2003), the definition offered by NLS presents literacy as something someone does in a domain, such as at school, at home, or in the workplace. The different domains in which literacies occur likely involve reading and writing, but this reading and writing is exclusive to that area, to that mode of operation. The types of communication in these domains are dependent on the situation—the norms for behavior and composition styles alter by space. People can be adept in some domains, possessing fluency in what Gee (2015) calls the Discourse of those fields, while knowing little about others. For example, there is a literacy involved specifically with Facebooking, a literacy in being a firefighter, a literacy in yoga. There are terms and ways of being specific to these fields. A student would not generally post on Facebook a completed essay written in Standard English on the merits of technology in the 21st century, but she would submit that same essay to a professor in a digital technology course.

All humans have multiple literacies, and their strengths within these can vary based on what they know, have acquired, or have learned about the particularities of that space. I would be lost in a yoga class, for example, but I read, discuss, and perform in other athletic domains daily, such as running. Literacies in teaching for social justice occur within the domain of the classroom and they are specific to the teacher, the space, and the nature of the oppression they intend to fight. Teachers who work for social justice exhibit various literacies based on their experiences, the students they teach, and their interactions with and knowledge of the world around them. Therefore, if literacies are social practices that can be taught and acquired, then it follows that the ways teachers act for social justice within their schools and classrooms can be described as literacies, and more importantly, they can be learned. What I aspire to throughout this book is first to provide examples of how English educators can position themselves to be open to learning such social justice practices and then to analyze instances of teachers who demonstrate these varied literacies of acting for social justice. I aim to explore how it is that social justice can appear in classrooms every day.

## SOCIAL JUSTICE: FOR WHOM AND BY WHOM?

It would be remiss to embark on the task of social justice in English classrooms without taking into account who it is teachers are and for whom they work as well as how that affects the nature of equity teaching. I will return more fully to the question of who teachers are in the subsequent chapter, but it is crucial to first note that the large majority of preservice and practicing English teachers are White, female, middle class, and heterosexual (Boser, 2014). Students in secondary classrooms, however, are diverse and range over a spectrum of ethnicities, social classes, and sexual orientations. These variations are even more pronounced across geographic location, where some schools contain predominantly White populations while others are principally students of color.

While many education scholars have cited the discrepancy between teachers and students as a reason we need culturally responsive and justice oriented education, and while I agree that there is certainly a need to facilitate preservice students' recognition of their backgrounds, I am hesitant to name this as the primary reason for social justice–based education, because doing so runs the risk of centering whiteness (Matias & Zembylas, 2014). We do not need social justice simply because teachers are White. We need social justice because oppression is prevalent in our society. This justification also "perpetuates the myth that antiracism work only benefits children of color—when in actuality, engaging in a critical praxis improves the livelihood for all" (Bausell, 2017). Furthermore, such a sentiment carries the assumption that all teachers of one race, class, gender, and sexual orientation are the same, which we know cannot be true. Humans are complex individuals. To shift away from this angle, I argue that any person can—and should— strive toward an equity-oriented mindset and toil for the goals of justice with their students. No social group affiliation precludes a person from being able to do social justice or inherently affirms their capacity to do so.

Anti-oppressive pedagogies, then, can be accomplished by any teacher and in a wide range of circumstances. Yet educators' backgrounds will differ and will influence the topics that teachers choose and the methods with which they approach those topics. Teachers, three of whom I analyze in this book, have histories and experiences that lead them to focus on different elements of social justice or to undertake particular causes. A person might feel more inclined, because of her own experiences related to her ethnic makeup, to work with students on racial divides, while another may wish to focus on social class discrepancies as a result of her personal commitment to eradicating poverty. The context in which teachers work, with regard to student demographics, geography, and political climate, also greatly affects the ways they support their critical approaches. Furthermore, students' socializations might place them further along the scale of social justice knowledge

(Dyches & Boyd, 2017). They may need more or less information depending on their foundation of knowledge on a topic or event. There is, however, always room for growth, and all students have a right to a critical education regardless of their positions. As with all teaching, gaining access to our students' background knowledge related to social justice topics and working from there is key (miller, 2014).

Social justice, then, can and *should* differ by teacher and according to student population. North (2008) sheds light on this notion, stating that

> When some students are struggling to find food and shelter while others are debating the merits of this advanced placement class over that one, we cannot expect a single approach to social justice education to be effective for all students in all contexts. (p. 1200)

Differences in student populations might translate into starting points, as some may need to understand how privilege exists in society, while others may be more inclined to begin with an examination of a local issue that affects them. One student group, such as a predominately Muslim population, might necessitate a stronger focus on representation in the media because that most relates to their vested interest as members of a group ignored or distorted by the media (Mendez, 2014). Others, such as White students, might be more prone to study institutional patterns of oppression over time as members of a dominant group. Social justice then is first and foremost student-centered, and teachers enact their critical pedagogies with their student demographics in mind.

Given these possibilities, how is it possible to learn how to "do" social justice in a secondary English classroom? Truly, embodying equity education is a lifelong and career-long journey. Teachers can, however, learn from others as they embark on this path. Seeing the practices, triumphs, and struggles of those who came before, who teachers can perceive are, in many instances, "just like them," can be helpful as they navigate the terrain of implementing social justice teaching. Especially when the enactment of social justice teaching depends so largely on context, they can benefit from snapshots of teachers working with varied student populations and in differing districts to better see how they can adjust the components of equity pedagogies to the students in their classrooms.

This book, therefore, and the three teachers I examine within it, provides an understanding of how social justice can occur in diverse contexts and suggests how educators can adapt methods into their own practice. The educators whose pedagogies I analyze span from working in middle to high school grades and in rural to urban contexts. They work in environments with mixed levels of support from administration and parents, and they adjust to those levels in ways that are consistent with their own dispositions and personalities. Their individual classrooms illustrate distinctive manifestations of social justice in English pedagogies and provide content from which teachers can learn.

Studied collectively, the three educators I analyze reflect some commonalities in their equity orientations and exercises. Therefore, through careful examination of their practice, I believe there are assertions that can be made about what it means to teach for social justice in English classrooms. Teaching for social justice includes exposing all students, regardless of track placement, race, class, or gender, to curriculum that is rigorous, multicultural, and inclusive, *and* facilitating youth's skills for critique of their social worlds. It also involves utilizing pedagogies that cultivate students' abilities to dissect power relations and helping students locate themselves within these structures of power so that they can act for change.

Without labeling these shared aspects, it would be impossible to define social justice education and an "anything goes" mentality would reign. Social justice, built around reflection, critique, and action, is far from "anything goes" but has a specific agenda, as outlined above. I argue, therefore, that while social justice foci and pedagogies do differ by teacher and student population, the basic premises are similar across the board. The practices of the teachers I analyze in the remainder of this book demonstrate those localized aspects and build a more global picture of social justice education.

# CHAPTER 2

# The Teacher as a Catalyst for Social Justice

For an English teacher, a social justice stance often embodies what is known in the field as *critical literacy*. Critical literacy is the theoretically based practice of questioning the makeup of texts (broadly defined) for their implications of power, maintenance of the status quo, and reflection of dominant ideologies (Luke, 2000). Rooted in the work of Paulo Freire, a Brazilian educator who championed the right of oppressed and economically disadvantaged citizens in Brazil to an informative and transformative education, critical literacy is built upon a foundation of being critically conscious. Hinchey (2004) explains critical consciousness as "an awareness that our ideas come from a particular set of life experiences, an ability to trace our ideas to their sources in our experiences, and an acknowledgement that others will have equally valid, if different, life experiences and ideas" (p. 25). Following the work of Freire (1970), critical literacy scholars today encourage students to examine texts for their modes of production and reflection of meaning—to see that a text has been created by someone and for someone and upholds specific values, rather than being merely as a neutral entity (Janks, Dixon, Ferreira, Granville, & Newfield, 2013).

One popular example of a text we can read critically is the show *American Idol*. Produced by Europe's largest television company, the funding sources behind the show certainly relate to its instant sensational status. Furthermore, the show's success came in the aftermath of the attacks on U.S. soil on September 11, 2001. Not only did it appear at a time when Americans wanted to affirm their pride in their country, but the program also sustained the values of competition and fairness that Americans hold dear. It provided the quintessential demonstration of the American Dream— living rags-to-riches stories—before the audience's eyes. Thus, although on the surface *Idol* is an entertaining television program known to many, the possibilities for reading the show critically are vast. A critical consciousness is required to be able to seek out and understand such investigations of economic and historical contexts and to match social consequences to each. This example from popular culture shows that texts are not limited to Shakespeare or nonfiction books and that critical literacy can be applied to any part of our society. Practicing critical literacy is a constant interrogation, and it is not only a process to be lived by teachers with students in classrooms but also one that happens on a personal level. Teachers as human beings committed to social justice will learn that their critical consciousness, to some degree, is ever present.

## COMING TO KNOW OURSELVES

How do educators become these practitioners of critical literacy in all aspects of their lives? Coming to know who they are as socialized beings is a crucial first step in reading the world and being critical teachers. The experiences that have shaped them, both related to education and to their familial backgrounds, influence the way that teachers interpret events and filter information (Sensoy & DiAngelo, 2012). They might believe they should teach the way they were taught (Boyd, Gorham, Justice, & Anderson, 2013; Lortie, 1975), or they may interpret an event in a way that they think is obvious but which actually has another side they could not imagine. Perhaps most important, educators' experiences affect how they think about their students and their families and what expectations they have of them. This applies to thoughts about gender, sexuality, race, and social interactions.

Teachers must recognize that behaviors of students and their own expectations for them come from a particular context—they must develop their critical consciousness. And equally as important, they have to understand that *different does not equal deficit*. If teachers assume that someone who is unlike them is somehow lacking and that it is their job to fill that void, they run the risk of exhibiting the negative behaviors that they likely wish to eschew (Delpit, 1995; Gay, 2002). They should not want, for example, to create students who are replicas of themselves, because they should want to honor the uniqueness of youth. If teachers think, however, that students are missing the same cultural values that they have and initiate classroom procedures for instilling those, they have stripped adolescents of that individuality. The detriments of implementing even subconscious expectations or enacting microaggressions (Nadal, 2008) can have vast consequences for students, including disengagement from school.

How, though, can teachers come to know themselves, and how can they conceive of the ways in which their backgrounds will affect their teaching? One exercise I have found useful to bring to the forefront my own and my preservice teachers' socializations is to craft or locate five objects that answer this question: Who are you and from where do you come? These can be digital images, material artifacts, or artistic representations. Once these objects have been determined, the second phase of the activity involves analyzing them in terms of how they might arise in the individual's teaching. Imagining an example for each is helpful to fully discern how the artifact affects the person.

For instance, when I have completed this exercise with my teacher candidates one of my personal objects is an artistic representation of the state of North Carolina. Being from the South affects me in many ways, some of which I did not know until I moved out of that region. I consider myself critically conscious, but I did not realize that my experiences in the South had narrowed my scope of race primarily to issues of White, African American, and Latino groups. When I moved to Washington state and chose texts for my classroom, I realized I had excluded certain populations of students and thereby limited the conversations in my classroom on racial dynamics to those groups. My students, some of whom identify through Native American tribal affiliations and many of whom grew up on or near reservations, helped me see how my background influenced my teaching. Many preservice teachers, while completing this exercise, utilize objects to symbolize the religion to which they subscribe or in which they were raised. When considering how this will permeate their teaching, they share that it might shade the way they perceive family structures, how they interact with school colleagues, or even how they judge their students' choices. This provides the class with an opportunity to reaffirm that difference does not equal deficit.

I also consider, with my preservice candidates and using their objects, the elements of themselves that they can specifically tap into for social justice work, exploring what experiences each of them has had that might dispose them to work with others toward equity. These "social justice funds of knowledge" (miller, 2014) are critical; rather than perceiving teacher candidates as lacking, this follows a more recent trend in education that attempts to see teacher candidates in more additive ways, the manner in which teacher educators ask them to discern their own students. From this angle, my students share how the loss of family members has influenced their lives and how they might be able to work with students similarly afflicted. Many note their encounters with racism in their hometowns or schools and discuss how they will seek to employ anti-oppressive teaching strategies. No one is a blank slate waiting to be filled, and all teachers have experiences and knowledge that they can activate for social justice purposes. Activities such as this one help to bring those aspects to the forefront and consider how to harness those experiences in teaching.

Similar to the object exercise, other ways for teachers to get to know themselves and to relate their experiences to social justice can occur through autobiographical writing. I have worked with preservice teachers to develop educational autobiographies at the beginning of the semester and then to revisit them at the end of the semester (Boyd & Noblit, 2015). In this endeavor, candidates crafted multimedia presentations to note significant moments in their educational experiences and then were asked to extend and critique those submissions from a social justice angle, using course concepts, in a written reflection. One student shared an experience from a program for gifted students in which she was involved, and she later questioned the notion of ability-based groups in her second iteration. Other students shared moments in their initial submissions of being activists in their youth and later extended those in more nuanced ways, deeply examining who they advocated for and why. Reflective writing gives preservice and practicing educators not only a way to see themselves anew but also a way to envision themselves for their futures.

## THREE TEACHERS' STORIES

The teachers whose practice I investigate in the remainder of this book have all engaged in their own self-reflection and have located in their own stories pivotal moments when their critical consciousness developed. Although each teacher represents a unique positionality in terms of racial background, sexual orientation, and general life experience, they all connect those to their motivations for teaching and to the specific causes they advocate. While their paths to equity-oriented teaching are distinct, they similarly harness difficulties they encountered in their personal circumstances, such as having faced ethnic discrimination or being a member of a marginalized group, to work for a more just society with their students. They also note influential figures from their early years, including their own teachers and parents, as key to their knowledge of equity, and they highlight how their individual interests in critical topics and characteristics of their own personalities inform their approaches.

In the narrative of each teacher, the way she defines social justice directly relates to what she wants for her students and to the kinds of adults she wants them to become. This includes a desire for youth to become more critical thinkers or to attain a solid education despite their social circumstances that can be barriers to learning. Although the teachers work in varied settings and with assorted content material, all three reveal goals that cater explicitly to the youth who are in their classes—they solicit resources and incorporate perspectives that speak to the demographics and interests of those individuals. They set up their classroom environments in ways that illustrate not only their individual personalities as educators and as people, but the aesthetics of their classrooms also communicate their philosophies on justice to their students. I argue that by studying across the stories of these three teachers and comparing their contexts and journeys it becomes more clear how social justice can be undertaken and adapted by any teacher under any set of circumstances.

## Etta Swan[1]

*Etta's School.* Etta Swan is a second-year high school teacher at Pacific High School, located in Pacific County on the coast of a southeastern state. Students attend her school from three clustered towns: Riverview, Bankston, and Tall Oaks. The three areas have 13,550 permanent residents collectively and all largely depend on tourism as their main industry, boasting roughly 40,000 visitors in the summer months. They are charming small towns, full of shops and restaurants located directly on the scenic waterway. Tall Oaks, the area immediately surrounding the school, is smaller and has a more rural feel. Taken together, the population of the region is predominately White (> 75%), yet there is a wider discrepancy in social class because the fishing industry intersects with local power-plant workers and commuters who make the 30–45 minute journey to the closest metropolitan area where they work in hospitals, law firms, and similarly situated occupations. The median income for a household in Bankston is $40,496 and for Riverview and Tall Oaks it is $32,399 and $28,406, respectively.

Pacific High School reflects these demographics. In a county with only two other high schools and district enrollment of 12,500 students in its 21 total schools, the student body at Pacific is approximately 1,100, with a population that is 78% White, 19.5% Black, 2% Hispanic, and .5% Native American. There are 77 classroom teachers in the school, and with the exclusion of Etta, who identifies as mixed-race, all of the remaining teachers are White. Of the four school administrators, three are White women and one is a White male. Although the school has had a few teachers of color over the last few years, many went into administration both in Pacific and other counties. The school was left with a student body that is somewhat diverse and a teaching force that is completely monolithic and monocultural, which is reflective of the population of teachers at large across the United States (Boser, 2014).

There is a relatively positive and participatory school culture at Pacific High. For instance, during Homecoming Week, the student council selects themes for each day and students are encouraged to dress accordingly. The week includes days such as "Team [sports affiliations] Day," "Decade Day," and "Class Day," the last of which is a day each grade is assigned a particular color to wear. On "Camo Day," many students don their camouflage gear, which includes hunting suits, ball caps, and boots. The influence of local churches and businesses at the school is also apparent, as religious organizations donate gifts and supplies for teachers throughout the year and sponsor lunches for school staff. Etta's desk houses a small flowerpot with a paper attached that reads: "Welcome back. We love you and we support you! Cross United Methodist Church." There is a huge billboard, visible from the school, that contains advertisements for sponsors who donate

---

1. All references to teachers, schools, students, and places in this book are pseudonyms.

financial support to the school's athletic teams. Thus there is a genuine sense of community involvement in the school.

Aside from these encouraging elements of student and community culture, there is conversely an element of pessimism in the culture of school staff. Teacher turnover is at a high with at least 10 teachers having left to seek employment elsewhere in the last year, often as a result of low wages and the need to support families, or when opportunities arose that were more lucrative and lured educators from the profession. In fact, a teacher who was a finalist for State Teacher of the Year resigned to take a more profitable position in education. Teachers are feeling downtrodden by local news coverage of effective teachers leaving the profession. As a whole, state policies in this right-to-work state, including the legislature's elimination of the potential for new teachers to earn tenure, are not favorable for education in general. Teachers' salaries have not increased in several years, and the state ranks amongst the bottom 10 in the nation in teachers' pay. Constant budget cuts threaten the existence of music and art in the state's schools. Pacific High is undergoing a shift in administration to its second new principal in 3 years. The transference fostered new local procedures and dismantled former practices that the teachers found efficient. Thus, the overall attitude is one of uncertainty, and teachers meet these changes with reluctance.

*Etta's Classroom.* Despite this general melancholy, walking into Etta Swan's classroom feels like being embraced in a warm hug. It is a friendly place, bustling with action and humming with the chatter of adolescence. It is often difficult to locate Etta among her students. She is barely 5 feet tall with a petite frame. Her long dark hair, youthful clothing, and trendy glasses cause her to blend in with the crowd, and her generally soft-spoken demeanor does not draw immediate attention. Yet somehow, once spotted, she fills the large room with her caring presence.

In her classroom, the desks are aligned in a large U, divided in half by a technology cart in the middle of the room. All desks are facing the front of this massive rectangular room, which sits on the perimeter of the courtyard where students are allowed to eat lunch. Etta teaches two classes of English I, which is a survey of various literary genres, to high school freshmen in the "standard" track, and one class of English II, which is a world literature course, to sophomore students in the "honors" track. Generally speaking, most classes at Pacific average 25 students who are mostly White. Etta's Honors English II class, for example, is composed of 21 students, with 16 identifying as White, 4 as Black, and 1 as Asian Indian.

*Etta's Social Justice Story: "I Can't Turn It Off."* Etta Swan is openly committed to social justice. She is passionate about issues of equity and has experienced a profound shift in thinking from a "white savior" mentality, wanting to rescue minoritized students as she had seen in so many Hollywood films, such as *Freedom Writers,* to a more critical and practical stance during her teacher education program. Once she entered the field, she negotiated her viewpoints with the reality of students' lives and the demands that came with having a multitude of students.

Etta's reasons for working for social justice stem largely from her ethnicity and her biographical experiences. She was born to a White mother and an Iranian father, and she lived the early part of her life in a metropolitan area where she attended ethnically diverse schools. In December of 2001, in the wake of the tragedy of September 11, she moved from urban Lee City to rural Pacific County. She describes this change:

> It was an interesting transition from being in a diverse population where my background wasn't really a big deal and then moving here where it very much was a big deal. So that was the biggest difference was just um (long pause) I was pretty terrified the first day of school because I had never seen so many people that were all of the same race. And that was hard. Which I know, I feel like most people talk about that with a flip to it, but . . . .

Once her family moved, Etta became painfully aware of her own ethnic makeup and, as she says, gained a "clear concept of what my race meant." Etta was subject to discriminatory remarks about her ethnicity that were hurtful. She remembers that a teacher introduced her sister to her new classmates as "Iranian, but not a terrorist." However, once she reached high school she had several teachers who sensed the way she was treated by peers and disrupted this negativity. She was deeply affected by those teachers, and a combination of her middle and high school educators inspired her to choose their profession as her own. She explains, "I had already been thinking about being a teacher in part because I wanted to be a different kind of teacher than what I had gotten, but then when I got to high school it was like no this is the type of teacher that I could be. And that was really cool."

Etta's social justice manifested from her own pain as a student. Her sense of unfairness came from her own experience with discrimination, and teaching is her avenue to heal her personal pain as well as to protect others from experiencing similar agony. She takes it on as her role to safeguard others, particularly her students who identify as LGBTQIA (Lesbian, Gay, Bisexual, Transgender, Queer, Intersex, or Asexual), from prejudices. In addition to these experiences surrounding her ethnicity, Etta attributes her social justice beliefs to other areas of her personal interests. As a self-proclaimed feminist, she feels that this part of her identity originated from the models of dependent women she witnessed while growing up. She thus feels that her critical consciousness began at a young age:

> When I was a little kid, when I was a little girl, I really liked the idea of girl power, but I think I took it a little bit more seriously than my friends did

and I learned that very quickly. I always had a sense that something wasn't right, but I couldn't figure out what it was. And for a long time I thought I was just crazy. I thought I just saw things that, to me they didn't seem right but they were normal.

However, once she attended a summer program for gifted high school students, she acquired a vocabulary for her thoughts, particularly the concepts related to feminism, and she returned home with a newfound sense of confidence and a place from which to speak.

As Etta continued her educational career in college and began her double major in women's studies and English, she was "hooked."

Women's studies just opens you up to all sorts of things. I mean . . . you're sort of looking for what's problematic and what's working and systems of power and oppression and all of that. And so then my brain was just turned on, and now I can't turn it off. Yeah, I don't know how to turn it off.

Following her women's studies and English undergraduate coursework, Etta entered a master's in teaching program. She affirms that the program

Gave me a really good lens for seeing my students as more than just students. And I felt like the little bit of ESL [English as a Second Language], like the ESL discussions that we had or discussions about LGBTQ students or just race and gender, and how I, just by being whoever I am, bring that baggage into my classroom and you know unpacking that invisible knapsack and all that stuff. I feel like the [program] gave me a way to think about my practice, that just being a teacher wouldn't automatically let you have. Because there's just no time. So I think that really benefitted me, a lot.

Beyond her courses, Etta's cooperating teacher in her internship was "completely on board with social justice, with questioning things," and Etta had opportunities to implement her ideals of social justice while in this phase of learning to teach.

Etta translates both the experiences from her upbringing and the knowledge and skills she gained in her undergraduate and graduate experiences to her teaching at Pacific High School.

I don't want to teach them what to think and I tell them that a lot. I just want to teach them—that sounds cheesy—but I just want to teach them how to think. And I just want to teach them how to question.

She focuses on the fact that many of her students in her rural area do not have experiences with people unlike them, and she wants them to learn

First and foremost . . . to be kind . . . and how to have a conversation with somebody and share what you think and to be a critical thinker. . . . So I think the most important thing is just to help them see that there are different opinions and there are different, you know, contexts outside of their little world. And helping them communicate within it and question.

While her responses on questioning and critical thinking resonate with the tenets of social justice and critical literacy, she says specifically that *teaching* for social justice means "providing students with a language that they can use and also, I'm just giving them a safe space to learn." For her, social justice is both curriculum and pedagogy. It is giving students tangible terms they can use but it is also constructing a community of learners. Thus the manner with which she approaches social justice in her practice is personal for Etta, and this is evident in her teaching, to which I return in Chapter 3.

### Beverly Mitchell

*Beverly's School.* James Middle School is located in metropolitan Apple City in the southeast region of the United States. With a population of 451,066 and a median household income of $46,612, Apple City is a rapidly growing area with sprawling suburbs and increasing ethnic diversity. Several universities operate within the city and nearby, and it is home to numerous cultural centers, sporting arenas, and historic sites. The estimated enrollment for the school district is 153,000 students in their 169 schools.

With its 1,214 students, James Middle is much larger than the national average of 575. Student demographics are reflective of Apple City and are approximately 58% Black, 21% White, 15% Hispanic, 5% Asian, and less than 1% Native American. Despite this range in student body, the 76 members of the instructional staff at the school are predominately White. The students consist of a mixed group: those who apply to and are selected for the school's dual magnet program based around arts instruction; those who participate in an International Baccalaureate (IB) track that boasts interdisciplinary learning, inquiry-based teaching, and global awareness; and those who have been assigned to James Middle because of their location in the district. The district constructed the magnet program and placed it in an area with lower socioeconomic status to attract students during a controversial busing movement that was designed to integrate school communities along economic divisions. Thus, in one sense the school population pulls from a variety of areas, and in another, the school population reflects the local, urban community. Students in Beverly's classes are predominately from the latter situation, having been appointed to the school from the local area.

James Middle advertises a very direct and specific mission. Posters lining the hallways display the slogan "The Way We Do Business at James Middle School," and teachers are expected to follow this prescription and hold their students accountable throughout the year. Students' knowledge of the policy begins with their teachers' delivery of a PowerPoint presentation in the first week of school that outlines expectations and school rules and sets the tone for the school culture. The two major school campaigns are "Oh, the places you will go if you dare to" and "Make it right, don't fight." There is a sharp intolerance for bullying and gang activity. Specific components of the behavior regimen in the school literature include what to do when an adult speaks in front of the room, stating that students should "stop talking and moving" and raise their hands until they "see the speaker drop their hand and begin talking."

The school provides students with agendas in which to write their homework daily and teachers are expected to sign these each day as a way to document homework and communicate to parents. There are rules and procedures listed and posted in the school (as well as in the introductory PowerPoint) for the cafeteria, media center, bus loop, bathrooms, hallways, and after-school activities. No food or drink is allowed in classroom spaces. As a whole, the school presents itself as unified in a strict approach to student conduct.

There is a high rate of teacher turnover at James Middle, and the entire 7th grade English Language Arts team of teachers is new this year. The general sentiment at the school is one of genuine care for student success. This is combined with a high level of expectation for student behavior based on the strict policies previously mentioned.

*Beverly's Classroom.* Beverly Mitchell thinks of her teaching persona as "quirky and fun for the kids," characteristics which she reveals in her classroom design. She lines her walls with posters, quotes, and charts, almost all of which she made, that relate to her course content. For instance, she posted alphabetical letters to construct the quote, "A word after a word after a word is power" by Margaret Atwood, meant to inspire students through an emphasis on speaking and writing, which they do daily in her class.

Beverly's space mirrors her sense of care matched with the strict expectations in the broader school culture. She arranges the desks in her room in groups of four, where students sit facing one another. Four computers track the back wall, but none are in workable condition and all possess signs noting their broken state. There is a small bookcase in one corner that contains a number of texts written for adolescents, and there is a student desk partitioned off and facing the wall in the corner of the room. Beverly uses this desk for students designated a "time out" by teachers in other classrooms, or for students whom she feels need to be separated from their peers. A long row of shelves leading up to the library case holds bins for each class period where students file graded work. Above those hang colored paper balls for decoration.

In addition to these elements, the whiteboards in the room illustrate this teacher's conscientious organization as well as the various components of her pedagogic strategies. For instance, Beverly guides her units by an "Inquiry Question," which is written on the board and is a broad query to which Beverly directs class readings and connects social justice topics. The question now posted reads, "What does it mean to come of age?" In addition to that component, Beverly's board reflects the school's IB mission to promote a "Global Context," the heading under which she has written the words "Fairness & Development." Students' scores on weekly quizzes on sets of morphemes, averaged and differentiated by class period, are recorded on charts that hang above the board. Homework is written on the right section of this board, and the procedure for "give me five" (what to do when an adult is speaking) hangs above the main board. Beyond these elements, another section of the wall contains the classroom rules, which support school policies and clearly communicate student behavioral expectations. Again, Beverly's tangible classroom materials and setup illustrate aspects of her social justice pedagogies, to which I will return more fully in Chapter 4.

Beverly teaches 6 class periods of 8th grade English Language Arts. These include 2 classes labeled "Inclusion," in which a specialist joins her for instruction and behavior management, 2 classes labeled "Academically and Intellectually Gifted" (AIG), and 2 classes labeled "Standard." The numbers of students in each class fluctuate over the year. There are 21 students in both her AIG and Inclusion classes and 16 students in the Standard class. The students in all of Beverly's classes are predominately African American or Latino. Eight out of 21 in the AIG class are White. Despite the variation in tracks, Beverly implements the same lesson plan and teaches the same texts, with few minor adjustments, across all classes. She feels the variation within her classes is actually greater than between them and, in an attempt to meet the needs of her students and to be more equitable, she endeavors to use the same texts.

*Beverly's Social Justice Story: "Putting in the Extra Effort."* Beverly's belief in social justice developed as she grew up both in diverse schools and with parents who openly discussed and supported social issues at home. A White, 31-year-old female, she was born in what she characterizes as a diverse city, and she attended a public elementary school that she felt was equally diverse. Her first high school, however, felt less socioeconomically stratified, and before she entered 11th grade her family moved to a different city where her new high school was less racially diverse but was more so with regard to family income levels. These experiences culminated in an overall exposure to a variety of people. She attended high school in the era of celebratory multicultural discourse in education (Banks, 2010), and Beverly realized in her youth that it was impractical to pretend that a person's race did not exist.

That's the time period when talking about issues of race was all about like you should not acknowledge race or be aware of race and it's like all color-blind kind of stuff. So you know, I always, I always liked to think about that and struggle with that as a kid, and I'm glad that was a ridiculous thing to try to deal with because it's impossible to do, right?

Her awareness of race despite the dominant narrative generated from personal experience. As an adolescent, she had an African American friend whose parents did not allow her to attend Beverly's birthday party. While she had friends of different races in school, they did not "hang out outside of school because we lived in different neighborhoods and one of them wasn't allowed to hang out with me." Beverly spent a lot of time reflecting on why those separate spheres existed and on truly understanding why her friend's parents might have felt as they did. This deeply affected her, thus she began building the perceptions of difference at a young age.

Coupled with these experiences were those that her parents intentionally cultivated for her. Having grown up in rural Mississippi during the civil rights era, Beverly's parents held to liberal politics based on what they witnessed in their own youth. As a result, they involved Beverly in activities that would promote her growth and critical outlook:

Well, my mom was a teacher and now works as a religious educator but is just really concerned with social justice in general and does a lot of volunteer work. Like as a kid we would go to the battered women's shelter and I would hang out with the kids and she would like watch them while they were having their group meetings and stuff like that. So those kinds of things. And I felt like very comfortable talking about those issues at home.

Teaching is a second career for Beverly; she earned a master's degree in creative writing and worked in the publishing sector prior to completing her degree in education. Again influenced by her mom, who taught her that "doing something that's good for society versus making a lot of money" is more important, she decided to become a secondary English teacher. She feels that her work in publishing was not stimulating and that she was not contributing to society. She contrasts this with teaching, which offers the "autonomy of the classroom" and allows her to feel, as she says, "like I am doing something every day." For her, teaching is a way to make "the world a better place." Her reasons for teaching include the independence she sees that the profession offers and her interest in influencing students' lives.

Beverly affirms that for her, the most important lessons for her students are not necessarily content related but are about working through the system of school and gleaning "life lessons" about "the bigger picture." To her, teaching for social justice means

That every kid will get the same thing from the class. In the sense that a kid who needs more will get more from me. Equity. And a kid that doesn't need as much will get everything that I should give them and like I still have a relationship with them, but I think a lot of times that means putting in the extra effort with kids who need it.

She recognizes that it is easier for her to connect with students who are similar to her. However, "the relationships with the kids who you don't bond with right away are more beneficial to you and to them because you're learning how to deal with people who are different from you." She feels her advanced students are "good at school," because they hold the knowledge that is deemed valuable before entering school. She attempts to work within the structure that is in place and from where her students are when they enter her classroom. Finally, she considers as part of her job being a positive adult influence for students so that they can prudently navigate the world in which they live.

Beverly identifies her colleagues as also disposed toward social justice and sees the whole climate of her school as centered on related issues. Although James is "a hard place" to teach and the teachers are "overwhelmed and exhausted," she is emphatic that the people who work there genuinely care about the students and their success and would not have chosen this environment if they thought otherwise. With regard to colleagues and collaboration, then, Beverly perceives a supportive context and feels that all are congruent with the fundamental mission of the school. Her focus for social justice then is on knowing her students and establishing relationships with them so that she can help them achieve success in society at large.

### Tate Williams

*Tate's School.* Ivy Middle School is located in the city of Harperville in a state in the southeastern region of the United States. Harperville is an urban area with a population of 228,330 and a median household income of $47,394. The city's story includes its fame as a site for events during the civil rights movement of the late 1950s and early 1960s. Historically, its population consisted largely of African American citizens and the area was home to sit-in demonstrations and notable leaders. Dr. Martin Luther King, Jr., visited the city several times during the era to deliver his message of nonviolent protest. The school systems were not separate from this fight for justice, and the National Association for the Advancement of Colored People was active in achieving desegregation in Harperville schools by 1970.

Although the large school district boasts a host of magnet programs and specialized schools, this middle school houses traditional courses and standard curricula. Fifteen percent of the school population has been identified with special needs, and the school employs the accompanying support staff to serve those students. Administrators organize grade levels into teams of teachers and designate specific teams for students with special needs. The school also offers classes solely for second language students and (separately) for students who do not speak any English. The mission at the school is focused on global connections and emphasizes maximizing students' potential to become productive members of society. The cafeteria and the library are lined with flags from countries all over the world in an effort to demonstrate their global emphasis, and bulletin boards in the hallway also promote this purpose.

The total number of students attending Ivy Middle is 1,320. The school reflects the diversity of the larger population of the city of Harperville with a student body that is 52% Black or African American, 32% White, 13% Hispanic, and 2% Asian. There are approximately 73 teachers who are overwhelmingly White and female. Although the general education teachers are mostly White, almost all of the elective teachers, such as those who teach dance, chorus, or art, are women of color. There are four administrators, all of whom are African American. The principal and one assistant principal are African American females, and the other two assistant principals are African American males.

Tate says Ivy Middle School's student population reflects the "haves and have nots," two groups between which she discerns an apparent line. Sixty-four percent of the student population receives free or reduced lunch and general passing rates on the End of Grade tests are 39% across discipline areas. Twenty-four percent of students are enrolled in the Academically and Intellectually Gifted (AIG) program, and parents of these students are vocal in the school in terms of their communication with teachers and in their involvement in groups such as the Parent–Teacher Organization. Despite passing rates, school administrators mandate that teachers offer tutoring for students who received a level 3 on the standardized test in the previous year, in hopes that they will earn a 4, the highest level attainable, on the test given at the end of this school year. There is a push for the upper echelon to rise higher while the demarcation between the two groups remains stark.

*Tate's Classroom.* Tate Williams' classroom is a vibrant place. Decoration, organization, and use of space draw the eye in several directions. Desks are arranged in pods of four or five, and above each arrangement hangs a colorful sign from the ceiling that displays a number. This number denotes the group to which the configuration of students who sit underneath it belong. Tate references these group numbers throughout instruction, class discussion, and assignments, and she also uses them to dismiss students from class. These groups are the basis of her building classroom community, as students learn to work closely with their assigned peers.

In the back left of the room is a "Reading Corner," with sofas and a student book library organized by genre. There is a sign on one of the couches that instructs students that they are only allowed to enter the reading corner when given permission from Ms. Williams. Students enter the reading corner at various times of the day—sometimes during Tate's class and at other times when they are sent from another teacher's room to Tate's. This cozy corner is a refuge for students among traditional school structures. The books in the library span an assortment of genres, including young adult literature.

Other key components of the classroom that communicate Tate's philosophy are the posted rules, which resulted in the acronym "Grrr" and personify the school's mascot, a cougar. The rules include students treating one another in accordance with the "Golden Rule," and being "Respectful," "Responsible," and "Ready." Tate's calendar on the wall displays what students should expect during the week, including school events and daily homework. She keeps a log on the wall that instructs students where certain class activities should be located in their binders, and she adds to this regularly. A homemade poster on the wall reads,

Let's eat Grandpa
Let's eat, Grandpa
Correct Punctuation Saves Lives.

Tate teaches four classes of 8th-grade English Language Arts. Two of them are labeled exceptional children's (EC) classes, denoting that most of the students in them have Individualized Education Plans (IEPs) and 504s, or federally legislated plans for modifications for students with special needs. In these classes with Tate there is often an inclusion teacher and a behavior specialist, who provide one-on-one support for the students with special needs. One of Tate's other classes is composed of students all in the Academically and Intellectually Gifted program, and her final class is regarded as Standard level. These classes range from 25–30 students. First period for example, Tate's Standard class, contains approximately 25 students, almost all of whom are students of color. Second period, the AIG class, is composed of 32 students, the majority of whom are White. There are 8 students of color in that class.

*Tate's Social Justice Story: "Everybody Gets What They Need."* Tate's memories of her early schooling are limited. She attended elementary school where her mom was a teacher, which mostly affected her when her mom was her 5th grade teacher. The lineage of educators in her family is long and, for her, teaching seemed a natural career path. She grew up all over the state in her early years but settled into a suburban area permanently with her family in her 7th-grade year. Her recollections of middle and high school are punctuated by her membership in athletic teams.

Tate has more vivid memories of her high school experience, during which she was student council president and was enrolled in honors and advanced placement courses. She speculates that the student population at her high school was 60% Black and 40% White. She remembers encountering three school lockdowns during her freshman year because of gang fights but discloses that she was oblivious at the time to the severity of the situations. Because she was around gangs in her high school and had friends whose brothers were in gangs, she feels "it's not that big of a deal" that some of her current students are involved with gangs and explains, "it doesn't necessarily freak me out." Because she had known gang-affiliated people in her youth, she gained an understanding of the need to belong and to survive, and she has a sense of appreciation for her students and their families that she may not have assumed otherwise.

Tate also feels that she is able to connect with her students through her experiences with her sexual orientation. Tate identifies as lesbian. Although she does not elaborate extensively on this part of her identity in the story of her youth or its connection to how she became disposed toward social justice issues, this position became crucial to the way she presently works with students. She connects her approach to her own positionality:

> I've always kind of been drawn to minorities. Just because I feel like I also identify as a minority group because I'm a lesbian. And I feel like I don't fit into heteronormative society, which is such a major—like it's an overwhelming majority, that I am in turn drawn to other minorities. Not just sexuality, but race as well. And I just want, it's like rooting for the underdog, like I just want to understand, and I want to help, and I want to, you know like I want to empathize and I don't know, I just want to feel like they, I want to help them feel like they're not alone. And that somebody understands.

In particular, Tate identifies three experiences and people from her background that affected her outlook and culminate in her perspectives on racial issues. The first is having been raised a Jehovah's Witness:

> Something good that came from my religion . . . besides all the horrible and terrible no good very bad things, I always noticed that there was no differentiation between the White and Black people. There was an even mix, like we all sat together, we all still called each other brother and sister, regardless of race. And it was the first time that I saw mixed couples. Like a Black woman and a White man and White man and Black woman. And I think that from an early age just being around that you learn that it's like ok, cool. Because there is so much in society telling you that that's not right and that that's not a good thing, but if you see it from an early age that actually it's fine, it's not that big of a deal. I think that you're kind of desensitized to society telling you that it's not ok. . . . So I think at an early age I was exposed to different races and being ok with different races intermingling. And it wasn't different. There was nothing different about those two people except their skin color.

Tate is cautious to say that hers is a "basic understanding" of race that she formed at an early age in her religious experience. She recognizes that although people of different races are not inherently disparate, their race as a social construct carries real consequences. She took her original understanding of race as skin color variance and carried it through life as she met and worked with new individuals in college and at jobs, and this informs her relationships in teaching.

Another monumental experience central to Tate's social justice biography is her time as the only White player for 2 years on her high school girls' basketball team. Her teammates nicknamed her "white chocolate" because they said she was Black on the inside and White on the outside. She felt her experiences with her teammates helped her relate better to her Black students and taught her that "there's Black people and there's White people and there's no difference between the two of them. Just like, they have different families. Everybody has different families." Playing sports taught her to recognize difference while simultaneously showing her, as did being raised a Jehovah's Witness, that difference did not naturally equate to a negative opinion of those who were distinctive from her.

Finally, Tate remembers one teacher specifically who pushed the boundaries of her thinking and motivated her to focus on English. This teacher was "overtly liberal" and provided Tate's first exposure to an ideology with which she had not been familiar. Tate's school was very segregated, and Ms. Wentworth encouraged Tate to cross divides and to be a model for others. Conversations that Tate had with this teacher about racial issues remain with her, and Tate felt constantly supported in questioning social divisions. Not only did this teacher affect Tate's thinking about social justice, but the teacher was also a catalyst for Tate choosing to teach English literature. Ms. Wentworth "had a way of making it seem like it was really important that you read. . . . You have to read to make yourself a better person basically." Her emphasis on texts inspired Tate to carry the same prominence in her own teaching and to choose books in which her students would be genuinely interested.

Tate conceptualizes social justice as

Making sure that the way that I teach my students, the way that I present my information is accessible to everyone. Like the skills that I want my students to learn, all the students have a way of accessing that material. Which would require me to present in lots of different ways. Basically making sure that every student gets what they need, but that, I mean that is all over the board. . . . On a smaller scale, I do that with my students individually, like they need discipline in a different way, they need, you know? Like little things like that. I would say social justice is ensuring that everybody gets what they need in a way that they need it. Through my eyes as a teacher.

I treat, I honestly treat all of my students differently. Depending on their needs, depending on their background, depending on their IEPs, their

504s, depending on their mom yelled at them that morning. Like it's just so important the more that you know your students, the better you can serve them. Cause you have to serve everyone differently.

Tate emphasizes attention to students' individuality as central to social justice practice. She refers to this in terms of both students' academic needs as well as their socioemotional needs, and she identifies that it is a monumental task to get to know all students. Yet it is one that she feels is crucial. For Tate, then, social justice is about getting to know her students and their requisites and basing her interactions and instruction on that knowledge.

For Tate, attitudes and actions oriented toward equity, or social justice, are ubiquitous in her teaching:

> I mean I see it every day. I don't know exactly how I see it. The thing is I don't think about it. . . . It's every single day. In every single thing that we do. . . . I don't really think, I'm not really like "Oh my god, this is such an act of social justice" when I put this lesson plan together. I think it just kind of comes naturally.

Thus to her, social justice is an embedded mindset and practice, not something she necessarily always thinks consciously about. She feels that it is a way of being, and she does not separate social justice from who she is.

Tate's definition of social justice also reflects her commitment to a philosophy that acknowledges students' differential access to opportunities at a young age: "My AIG class came into school knowing how to read and write. You know? It's those fundamental years. . . . That kid knew their ABCs before they came to school, that kid doesn't." Thus, Tate sees the complicated and discrepant nature of students' admittance to school knowledge and its implications. Tate therefore expressed that the consequences of her students' opportunities before coming to her class were aspects she considers in designing and implementing her practices.

## INDIVIDUALIZING SOCIAL JUSTICE

Each of the teachers in this chapter describes how she developed a certain empathy for students based on her own experiences. Tate recognized race quickly when she was the only White girl on her high school basketball team. This experience forced her to see her own position in relation to others, and it translated into her teaching by helping her think about her students and their backgrounds. Etta's youth as a mixed-race female in a conservative, small town showed her what it was like to experience marginalization. Beverly's experiences of having friendships in her childhood with people of races different from her own, as well as working as a teen with populations with less opportunities, helped cultivate her disposition for social justice.

It is therefore the *experiences* of the teacher that are salient to developing her social justice practice, not necessarily her gender, race, or ethnicity. Kirkland (2008) writes that common among autobiographical narratives of social justice educators are "themes of passion and pain" (p. 61). Race alone, while decidedly an instrumental factor, does not fully equate to critical consciousness or to the capacity to work well with students on equity-oriented goals. The experiences of Etta, Beverly, and Tate led them to care about social justice. Yet each one's characteristics do not necessarily match her social justice focus. Etta is mixed-race, but she advocates most for her LGBTQIA students; Beverly is White and middle class but is concerned with her students' socioeconomic opportunities; and Tate identifies as lesbian but works to acknowledge race and inequities with her students. Thus, although qualities of their backgrounds may have oriented the teachers toward social justice, those are not necessarily the specific cause that they champion.

Once teachers determine their background and the strengths they bring to social justice teaching, they can also then establish which causes they will promote. These do not need to be static—social justice responds to the crises of the time and to the students in the actual classroom. Determining what is most important to the teacher and how to fit that into instruction is key. Knowing what interests students and which injustices they seek to address should also inform a teacher's pedagogies. Finally, ascertaining the potential limitations at school and deciding how to subvert while "working from within" (Urrieta, 2010) will be part of individualizing social justice for the teacher. Etta, Beverly, and Tate all mobilize their backgrounds and experiences to enact pedagogies that reflect themselves and their students while appreciating the greater context within which they work.

# Part II

# SOCIAL JUSTICE AND THE CLASSROOM

# CHAPTER 3

# Social Justice and Pedagogy
## Teaching with Purpose

Once teachers have begun to establish their own critical consciousness by reflecting on their experiences and distinguishing how those affect their approach to education, they can act in the classroom by employing methods for social justice teaching. This is not to say that a teacher should reflect and move on; reflection is an iterative process that should constantly inform teaching, and a person's critical consciousness is always evolving. Etta, Beverly, and Tate each describe how events in their backgrounds spawned their beliefs in equity and prompted them to work with their students in particular ways. Their reflections led them to conceptualize social justice uniquely and informed how they relate to the populations of students with which they work. They continue to learn and grow and to establish new practices with new students. Their methods, which are the focus of this chapter, are not only simply "good teaching" (Ladson-Billings, 1995), as some might initially think, but instead are pedagogies with the intent of dismantling oppression and inequity. Thus, in addition to the pieces that permeate a teacher's being who is committed to social justice, there are certain acts that characterize the practice of a social justice educator.

Those actions that distinguish teachers' social justice practices within the classroom are their literacies. They include occurrences such as reading the "texts" that are students and engaging with them in mutual, understanding relationships; utilizing language in disruptive and supportive ways; and demonstrating an ethic of care that balances rigor with understanding. Each of these methods involves a specific "know-how" that is honed throughout a teacher's career and thus can be learned and enriched over time, and each has a theoretical foundation that is rooted in fostering equity within the classroom and in a broader social sense.

## BUILDING RELATIONSHIPS FOR EQUITY

Building relationships with students is perhaps one of the most basic premises of any guide to successful teaching, as relationships imply that educators show a genuine interest in students that is reciprocated and that teachers cater curriculum to the individual interests and needs of students in order to foster learning. In teaching that is social justice oriented, however, there are more specific elements of these relationships. They are built in ways that promote equity and overtly attempt to dismantle oppression. Because of the inherent nature of the teacher–student dyad, it is not possible that these become completely horizontal relationships. Yet social justice educators do shift relational power dynamics typically found in schools because they value the student as a human being, outside of being a pupil. Likewise, the teacher shares her qualities and interests with the youth in her class. Teachers pay careful attention to privilege and power in their relationships, seeking not to favor dominant groups and working to provide space for students who have been historically marginalized. The point of origin for relationships with students is basic rapport—caring about students, talking with them, asking about their lives—yet other features involve teachers getting to know their students across boundaries and in terms related to culture (Moje & Hinchman, 2004), race, class, gender, and sexual orientation. They also comprise learning about students' special needs, their families and communities, and the environments in which they live. There are a number of components involved in building relationships that reflect social justice, therefore, and Etta exemplifies many of them.

## Advocating for Marginalized Students

Etta Swan is a staunch advocate for her students, especially for those who are not considered mainstream. Carmen, an African American student who identifies as a transgender female, was in one of Etta's classes early in her teaching career. Even though Carmen is no longer a student in her class, Etta continuously defends Carmen in the face of students and even other faculty who do not understand her or, worse, who latently or even sometimes overtly bully her.

> The bell rings between third and fourth period, and as Etta's fourth period files in, Carmen enters the classroom in a hurry to ask Etta if she can have a Band-Aid. Etta hurries to her closet in the back of the room to rummage through her first-aid kit, grabs a Band-Aid, hands it to her, and asks "What did you do?"
> "Oh, I just cut my finger," she answers. "Thank you!" and rushes out the door.
> A White female student a few rows back in the left corner, near Etta's desk, asks Etta, "How does he change his voice like that?"
> "What do you mean?" asks Etta.
> "I just think it would be hard to change your voice like that all day," the student says pejoratively.

Etta takes a moment, as if weighing the student's statement, and responds, "I don't think sheeeee [emphasized slowly] changes her voice, I think that's just her voice. And it's pretty cool."

"Oh [surprised sounding], yeah, ok, then," the student says, seemingly agreeing.

Did the student really agree with Etta? It's hard to know, but for the moment, Etta shows that she will not tolerate disparagement of Carmen in her class. Although the student's question was veiled as benign and as a genuine question (and perhaps it was meant as such), or even as a way to discern Etta's level of support of Carmen, Etta spins the concern into a positive so that the conversation cannot be molded otherwise. She continuously sets the tone toward Carmen in her current class and attempts to be a model for how she wishes her students will react to her.

Students are working on individual, school-owned laptops, searching for lyrics for their "Music as Poetry Project," an assignment in which they select a song of their choosing to analyze for poetic devices. They then create a multimedia presentation for the class to illustrate how these devices, such as metaphors and rhyme scheme, are used in the song. Students select a short clip of the song to play for the class during the presentation. They are eagerly searching and examining song lyrics. The classroom is quiet.

Kelly, a White female student, mumbles to her neighbor, "I might choose a song by Justin Bieber."

Carl, a White male student sitting a few rows away, comments offhandedly, "Justin Bieber is gay."

Immediately, Etta responds, "Oh, is Justin Bieber dating a guy?"

The class laughs.

Etta repeats, "I didn't know. Is he dating a guy?"

Carl says defensively, "I didn't mean it like that. I didn't mean anything bad by it. Carmen is gay or whatever and we are all cool with her."

"Ok wait, I would never let someone use you as an example in another class so we aren't going to do that here," Etta interjects. "Carmen isn't here to talk about herself."

Etta then launches into a conversation with students about choosing their words carefully. I will recount a similar discussion with regard to how Etta responds to the word "gay" being used in her class negatively in the next section. What I wish to point out here, however, is that Etta again advocates for Carmen. As in the previous scenario, the actual long-term effect on Carl is uncertain, but at least the seed has been planted for future thought and awareness before students speak negatively toward their transgender peer or even before they use expressions that are harmful. Despite the students thinking they are using Carmen, possibly the only student in the school who self-identifies as transgender, in a constructive light, Etta refuses to let them rely on a common trope used in society to escape prejudicial comments (e.g., "I have a gay friend, so I can't be homophobic"). She further solidifies her relationship with Carmen, but her expression that she would not allow this to happen to any of them (their being discussed in a class in which they are not present) inadvertently builds her relationship with them also. Seeing how she defends one student, others feel confident in her likelihood to also protect them if called upon.

In a number of other situations, such as when Carmen is being bullied on the bus and in the school courtyard during lunch, school staff come to Etta to solicit her insight and to mediate the situation. She is seen as the adult figure in the school who can assist them in understanding Carmen and negotiating proper punishment for the parties involved, including Carmen, when necessary. When students question Carmen's style of dress in the same way they do her voice, Etta is her protector, always embodying the ethic of acceptance as a standard for them. She says she gets a "momma bear instinct" when it comes to Carmen because she is an outlier in the school.

Even though she is no longer a student in Etta's class, Carmen stops by almost daily to say hello, to ask for supplies, or to give a report on an incident from the day (good or bad). Each time, Etta is warm, friendly, and helpful in whatever Carmen needs. It is quite evident when considering Etta's ability to build relationships that are socially just in nature with students that advocating for them, especially those who have the potential to be marginalized, inside and outside of the classroom, is a central part of her pedagogies.

## Appreciating the Range in Students' Positionalities

A central aspect of Etta's efforts to build relationships with all of her students is her ability to appreciate them for who they are, regardless of ability, diagnosis, or background, and she is inclusive of their personalities with all of their idiosyncrasies, political beliefs, and varied traits. Valuing students may seem, at cursory glance, an obvious inclusion—or even trivial and easy to do. However, genuinely accepting young people, especially if they are different from the teacher, and understanding students' motives while trying to maintain a cohesive classroom can be a challenge and can test the patience of the teacher.

One exemplary episode from Etta's class demonstrates her capacity for appreciating students:

> As students' read aloud from the play *Cyrano de Bergerac* (Rostand, 1985/1897) in parts, Etta pauses by the window where a row of desks are

aligned. Under one of the desks sits Megan, a usually loud, boisterous student, known in the school for her struggle with attention in her classes. Holding her book and following along, Megan looks up, brightly smiling at Ms. Swan. Stopping momentarily, Etta asks: "Megan, you ok?"

"Yep," Megan replies.

"Whatcha doing down there?"

"I'm just more comfortable here while we read," Megan responds nonchalantly.

The class laughs quietly.

"Ok," says Etta. "Keep reading, Julien," she instructs the student playing the part of Cyrano, and continues to circulate the room. The class returns to business as usual.

By allowing this student, Megan, to be who she is and by valuing her individuality, Etta shows her effort at establishing a relationship with her. Megan, following along in the book, shows that she is invested in what is happening in the moment, and thus in Etta as a teacher, and this relationship is reciprocated. Finally, Etta sets the tone for the rest of class by her reaction. Rather than reacting to Megan in a way that might connote she is "weird," or in any way turning the situation into a negative, Etta carries on. Just as she is the model for how she wants others, including students and her colleagues, to treat Carmen, Etta here sets the standard for how she wants others to treat Megan.

Why did Etta allow Megan to sit on the floor, under her desk? What would most teachers do in this situation? Etta explains her approach:

> It is this moment of—the same qualities—the qualities that Megan possesses that I love so much are the fact that she's so energetic, that she brings that positivity to my classroom— she is funny, she is engaged. Those are all positive attributes. And those are all the same qualities that made her sit under the table, in the middle of class. Because she is funny and she is energetic and she was engaged. . . I think she knows when she can and when she can't.

Etta never mentions Megan's labeled struggle with attention but rather focuses on the constructive elements of her personality. She makes clear her belief in being fair and equitable, but in her sense of these terms this means she has to value Megan's strengths *all* of the time. This is not just when they are convenient or when they fit the mold of traditional students, or even just when Etta feels like it. She also trusts Megan to determine the parameters for her own behavior, bestowing a sense of responsibility upon her.

Etta demonstrates this appreciation of students even in situations that lead to controversy:

At the school where Etta teaches, students stand and recite the Pledge of Allegiance every morning. Phillip, a White male student, doesn't stand while his peers complete the ritual. Etta says the pledge along with the class, taking no obvious notice of Phillip. Upon finishing the last line, delivered along with the student leader on the intercom, Nick, another White male, shouts at Phillip across several desks, "Come on man, can you just stand? At least show some respect!" The classroom becomes eerily quiet.

"There are more reasons not to stand than to stand," Phillip offers quietly.

Avery adds, "We were raised to stand and say the pledge. It's just what we're used to. Why would we change the words now?"

Etta intervenes, stating that "People have different perspectives on this," and explaining that her own mother is Jehovah's Witness and does not stand or say the pledge because of her beliefs about idolatry. When she begins to elaborate on the belief against worshipping an image or an object, Phillip interrupts her:

—"It doesn't have meaning for me," he says inaudibly—
— "I think we have to appreciate that we live in a country where we have the choice to stand," Etta finishes.

"Exactly," says Nick, "We have that choice because people have fought for us to have it. Have you seen *Saving Private Ryan*? I admit, I cried like a baby watching. But that's the people who gave us the option to stand. That's my opinion, and I think it's just kind of disrespectful."

Avery comments, "When you stand for the pledge you are saying you believe in something."

"I just don't really think there is liberty and justice for all," Phillip says, looking down at the ground.

"It's cool and brave of you both to share your opinion on this, you all, and it's ok if we disagree here. I'm ok with that," Etta tells them.

Nick then apologizes to the class and to Etta for shouting, and she affirms his right to his perspective as well as Phillip's right to his own. A short discussion ensues about this very divisive issue and Etta tells the class she is "proud" of them for being able to have a philosophic discussion at 8:00 A.M.

In this scenario, Etta enacts a number of social justice practices that relate to her building relationships with students. First, like Megan, Phillip here chooses to assert his individuality in Etta's classroom, and she acknowledges and validates him. Like in the case of Carmen, she advocates for Phillip instead of placing the burden on him to defend himself. It is obvious in the conversation that Phillip is not seeking conflict, and in fact is reluctant to speak at all. Etta supports him in a way that upholds her relationship with all of the students involved, affirming both Nick and Phillip and their beliefs in the context of the discussion.

Citing Barnes (1992), Smagorinsky (2007) differentiates between types of student participation in classroom discussions. The first, "*final-draft speech*," occurs in classrooms where "students are encouraged to participate only when they have arrived at a fairly well thought out idea that they can present to the teacher for approval" (p. 10). He matches this with types of teaching that reflect transmission, or the placement of knowledge into students' minds. *Final-draft speech* opposes "*exploratory* speech," which happens in constructivist classrooms, those in which students build knowledge in the moment. This type of participation is characterized when "students think aloud as they work through their ideas" (p. 11). The teacher is not the center of such a classroom but respects the voices of students.

In the scenario described above, students, particularly Nick and Avery, work through their thoughts aloud on the topic of the pledge. Avery's comments are almost contradictory, first wondering why anything should change with blindly standing and saying the pledge to then later realizing that standing does mean something. Nick is adamant in his first comment but then backs down a little as the discussion continues and apologizes for lashing out. By allowing them to "think aloud," from their own points of view and perspectives they bring with them to the classroom, Etta shows the students that she honors their opinions, although she also feels they should be open for exploration.

After class, Nick again apologizes to his teacher, having felt as though he started a conflict. That Nick cares enough to apologize illustrates that he values his relationship with Etta and does not wish to jeopardize it. In the days following, Phillip continues not to stand for the pledge, obviously feeling as though he is in a safe space where his politics are respected, even if not fully understood. There is no further discussion of the issue in class. The relationships that Etta maintains by allowing students to be themselves are thus observable. Other students affirm this aspect of Etta's relationship building, noting that she is able to bond with students across various personalities. One, for example, shares, "I just like her teaching method. It's like so, she relates with the students more." Thus, Megan and Phillip are only two of many instances of the ways that Etta accepts and welcomes students in order to build connections with them.

### Sharing with Students

Not only does Etta generally emanate a compassionate persona to maintain her relationships with students, but she also shares parts of herself with them, giving them a glimpse into who she is. In this sense, the relationship becomes more mutual and "when students know that someone cares about them, they more easily empathize with and even become excited about the

interests of that person; as a result, students are more likely to believe or
buy into a teacher's assertion that it is important to know some particular content-related generalization or a particular process" (Moje & Hinchman, 2004, pp. 339–340). Mutual sharing and solid relationships between
students and teachers, then, can actually increase student learning in the
classroom.

Etta's sharing occurs often. She generally communicates her interests to
students through personal stories that relate to topics of class discussion,
which usually generate from their study of a specific text. She references her
college experiences, her husband, and her friends frequently. She answers
students when they inquire about her Harry Potter tattoo, and she jokes
with them about her allegiance to her alma mater when they wear the rival
team's logo. These examples are woven seamlessly into her classroom pedagogies. Two patterns in Etta's sharing, however, are particularly salient to
her being oriented toward social justice.

Etta frequently provides examples for students that relate to her Iranian
roots. In her unit on human rights, Etta leads a discussion on diplomatic
solutions to the problem of countries that violate the human rights of their
own people. The conversation spans Rwanda, Syria, and Iran, and it refers
back to the students' reading of *Persepolis* (Satrapi, 2004) earlier in the year.
In the discussion, she articulates the following:

> I'll tell you what my Iranian family thinks right now. They're questioning
> their president because they've had a lot of unrest. They are super pessi-
> mistic right now. They are fed up and don't know what to think. But at the
> same time they are excited about the prospect of diplomatic relations. You
> have to remember that the government doesn't always do what the people
> want it to do.

In this instance, she uses her kinship to educate her students, but she does
so in a way that is personal.

Another related conversation occurs while students are reading Peggy
McIntosh's (1989) *White Privilege: Unpacking the Invisible Knapsack*. This
text, written by a White female, includes a catalogue of privileges bestowed
on the author simply because of the color of her skin. These are all things
commonly taken for granted by members of the dominant culture, such as
how prevalent members of their race are in magazines or how easy it is to
find Band-Aids that match their skin color. Etta uses her background to ex-
plain item 17 on the list, "I can talk with my mouth full and not have people
put this down to my color" (p. 10). She wants her students to grasp the ways
our society oversimplifies whole groups of people, so she expounds,

> It's like, when people find out my parents are divorced, they'll say, "Oh, is it
> because he (my dad) is Middle Eastern? Is it a cultural thing?" It would be
> like saying "all teachers wear red pants," because I am wearing red pants

today [she points to her trousers]. Does that make sense? If someone makes a misogynist joke, Owen, my husband, can say, "That was insensitive." But if I say it, people say "Oh, haha, that's Etta, she's a feminist."

Not only do students potentially learn something new here but they learn about their teacher simultaneously. She demonstrates the point that in education, "We teach what we are far more than we teach what we know" (Belmonte, 2003, p. 46). In this case, Etta's Iranian identity and cultural awareness are transparent to students.

In addition to her ethnic identity, Etta also uses her particular areas of interest as an entry point for teaching. She incorporates both her love of theater and her interest in popular music into her teaching. For example, Etta uses clips from *Legally Blonde: The Musical* (McCarthy-Miller & Mitchell, 2007), which she has seen onstage, to help students gain an understanding of the concepts of direct and indirect characterization. When students read *Cyrano de Bergerac* (Rostand, 1985/1897) as a class and act out parts, she teaches them theater techniques such as "blocking," which she knows from her past and current involvement with a local theater in which she takes parts in community plays throughout the year.

On a number of occasions, Etta uses lyrics from Macklemore songs as content for analysis, to draw a parallel to a character in a literary work or to illustrate a point related to the topic of study. What is noteworthy to her use here is that Macklemore is a highly controversial figure and that his lyrics may not be considered appropriate for a school context. Yet instead of shying away from him, Etta embraces these elements, acknowledges them in class, and continues to employ his music as a vehicle for teaching. Her keen interest in his music and her diligence in studying his lyrics afford Etta an opportunity to share Macklemore with her students and to use his songs for educational purposes. During her unit on Human Rights and Responsibilities, for example, Etta feels she cannot talk about human rights without talking about the rights of citizens in the United States. She introduces the concept of White privilege to her students through distributing copies of the uncensored lyrics of the Macklemore and Ryan Lewis song "A Wake" (2012). She plays the (uncensored) song aloud two times. In the song, Macklemore acknowledges his own privileges and offers a commentary on the music industry's reaction to his work. He believes this treatment is discriminatory, because as a White rapper he is praised for being poetic and articulate while other, predominately Black, rappers are condemned for the material of their songs. Students listen intently to the song and record notes on their papers. All eyes are on the screen in the front of the room as Etta shows them the website Rap Genius (2014), which elucidates lyrics and explains allusions.

Dallas asks, "Is he saying that Trayvon had to do with race?"

"Yeah, I think he is," Etta answers. "I think he's saying he wants to tweet

RIP but he doesn't want to make everybody uncomfortable and mad. So instead of doing anything about it and because of his White privilege and White guilt, he'll just party."

Mandy replies, "I think it's really disrespectful because if I was somebody that was related to Trayvon and I saw this about it I'd be mad."

"Yeah," Etta offers. "So I think what someone said earlier about it's just a tweet and everybody was doing it seems impersonal, but he says it might be emblematic of a larger issue so it might be important. And you may agree or disagree with that and it's ok."

The classroom conversation continues beyond Trayvon Martin, and students consider Macklemore's messages on teenage pregnancy, Reaganomics, and our culture's reliance on cell phones. By using her interests in Macklemore, Etta not only bolsters her side of relationship building wherein students get to know her interests, but she is able to connect to classroom material and promote social justice content.

As illustrated above, Etta engages in relationship building with her students throughout her classroom interactions. A social justice purpose undergirds each of her practices. She utilizes her skills for advocacy for her students, especially those from marginalized populations, as an ally and in order to be a model for her students as well as to negotiate with those in positions of power. Using her status as a teacher, she is able to ensure that Carmen has support at the administrative level. She allows students such as Megan and Phillip to be who they are, exhibiting practices that value their strengths, defining those as strengths at all times and not only when it is convenient. And, not only does she learn about her students, their personalities, and their stories, but she shares herself with them, demonstrating interpersonal practices, or those skills of reciprocation necessary to build multidirectional connections to others. These pedagogies, seen daily in her classroom, help to show how Etta engages in multiple explicit moves in her practice to bond with the youth in her classroom.

## EMBODYING TRANSFORMATIVE LANGUAGE PRACTICES

In addition to the myriad ways teachers can build relationships with students to work for social justice in their pedagogies, there are also, as Etta again demonstrates, discursive, or language-based, strategies that reflect equity approaches as well. Etta's use of inclusive language and connected nonverbal cues promote a particular mentality—one that upholds the ideals of social justice. Transformative language practices also involve disrupting language that is harmful, upholds stereotypes, or otherwise maintains oppression. We all, as humans, both reflect the world around us through our language and construct it; we use the words, symbols, and gestures we have learned over time, but we can also create new ones that have liberatory purposes, that change dominant narratives or overturn negative language use. The English classroom, a place where language and the study of it are continuous, is a prime spot for such pedagogy.

Whether we, as human beings, are conscious of it or not, our language reflects our beliefs as well as greater "social conventions, norms, and histories" (Fairclough, 2010, p. 57). These beliefs and areas may be something of which we are mindful—we know, for instance, if we use words that come from a particular geographic region (e.g., "ya'll") or even a certain generation (e.g., "groovy"). Most often, however, our language reflects values, knowledges, privileges, and prejudices that we take for granted or consider common sense. Think, for instance, of how we refer to social groups: What labels do we use? Where did we learn those? Why do we use certain terms and not others? Furthermore, how do we alter our word choices based on our audience—how do we "code switch" when we are speaking with a supervisor as opposed to a group of friends? What might we say in front of one that we wouldn't the other? Most of the ways we speak are innate, and without fully considering them, they might perpetuate social injustice in ways we do not intend.

The importance of language applies not only to the specific words we use but also to explanations (Dyches & Boyd, 2017) we give and the way we frame our responses to situations. For instance, if a student is struggling in school, does a teacher place the burden on the student, thinking they should work harder, reflecting the ideals of individualism and meritocracy? Or does she look beyond the student at the structure of the school that might not support the student fully, reflecting ideals of social responsibility? Does she say, "It's his fault" or "It's my fault"? The way individuals frame their immediate reactions to such situations says a lot about the principles they hold dear. Furthermore, conflicts related to language happen both overtly in schools, resulting from mismatches in how directives are given at home versus school (Heath, 1983), or implicitly, such as when teachers inaccurately judge the intelligence of their students based on language patterns (Delpit, 2008) or differentiate instruction and access to knowledge through their talk, exposing students to vocabulary or materials based on their perceived ability level (Cazden, 2001; Rymes, 2015). Yet, despite these few examples, not enough attention has been paid to the transformative language practices of social justice teachers for the ways they can use language to affirm and disrupt, and this is a crucial element in the habits of teachers who work for justice in their classrooms.

**Using Inclusive Language: Creating a "We"**

Etta Swan's pedagogies are rich with practices that reflect discourses for justice. She constructs a "we" mentality in the classroom, rather than one in which adolescents are seen as separate from the teacher. In both her verbal and nonverbal behaviors, she emanates attention to inclusivity.

Etta's establishment of the class as a positive, communal space begins the first day of school. On her syllabus for her courses, Etta includes a "Policy of Peace" that she asks students to sign. It reads:

> My main goal as a teacher is to create a *safe and welcoming learning environment for ALL of my students.* I cannot do that without a commitment from the entire class to strive for the same goal. I do not tolerate bullying of any kind. If you suspect bullying, please let me know. As a class and as individuals, we will respect and learn from our differences on all levels, including race, ethnicity, gender, nationality, creed, sexuality, gender expression, and belief system.

She reminds students of this policy when needed and especially repeats her goals to create and maintain a safe space when it is under threat. I return to this element below, but suffice it to say here that she places at the forefront of her teaching and communicates from the outset her beliefs in justice. Additionally, she includes another element in that initial conversation with her students:

> I also have them share their preferred gender pronoun[2] on the first day and I always say if this changes, let me know. If you have a preferred gender pronoun that you don't want me to say out loud and you just want me to know that that's your preferred gender pronoun, I do that. The kids who have one usually know, but I think in every class someone has said, "Hey Ms. Swan, what's a preferred gender pronoun?" and then we can have a conversation about it.

The discussions she has with her class then call for language that is respectful and identified by the students themselves.

There are also more nuanced ways in which Etta promotes an inclusive community through language. These occur in the ways she positions and speaks to her students. She almost always refers to each of her groups of students as "team" and rarely if ever uses the term "class." Finally, Etta often opens class by asking students for "highs and lows." In this exercise, students offer the best of what is happening in their lives and, if needed,

---

2. More recently, inclusive language trends have shifted from "preferred gender pronoun" to "correct gender pronoun." During the time I worked with Etta, "preferred" was recognized as the way to respectfully acknowledge individuals' gender identities.

pieces that are not going well for them. She also refers to this as "Happies and Crappies" and, again, it is a custom with which students are familiar. As soon as she mentions the phrase, students begin verbally sharing. Most often students share events such as succeeding in *Grand Theft Auto*, a PlayStation 3 game, and going to parties. Incidents categorized as "lows" are those including fights with guardians or getting in trouble at school. This pedagogic language practice therefore reinforces the communal nature of Etta's classroom.

### Disrupting Language: Challenging Words

Etta's use of affirmative language extends into moments of disruption as well. While the above scenarios recount positive, uplifting uses of language, our vocabulary has within it speech that is negative and perpetuates oppression. When moments of such uses arise in her classroom, Etta frames her discourse in ways that are still inclusive of her students but simultaneously disrupt narratives that are exclusionary and subjugate others:

> A group of 9th-grade students in Etta's classroom conclude their presentation on the book they've finished reading with their literature circle over the past several weeks. A student, Kesha, a White female, as a compliment to a group who has just shared their work, says,
> "Ya'll make all the other lit circle groups' work look gay."
> A chorus in the class shouts, "Find another word!" Familiar with Etta's posters on the walls and her stance toward derogatory language, they have taken to monitoring one another.
> "No, wait," Etta stops. "Let's talk about word choice in this situation. This is a word that is in our language as a habit. It's not Kesha's fault. It's habit. I don't think Kesha meant that the lit circles are interested in same-sex partners. What did she mean?"
> Kesha answers, "I meant they weren't as good as the one we just saw."
> "Ok, well you could have said they're uncool, I mean you know or poor quality or whatever. But if you use it as an insult—"
> Kesha interrupts, "I'm for gay rights. I support gay people."

Here Etta stops class to unpack this commonly heard language. As is characteristic of her teaching style, she shares a story from personal experience with her students to illustrate the potential damaging effects of the words they say:

> ". . . So that's great if you support gay rights, but let's examine your language a little bit. I have a friend named Jonah who is gay, and who was my really good friend in high school. I didn't know, and for a long time he was pretending to be homophobic and said all these things because when I was

in high school I didn't like when people said 'that's so gay' or whatever. Jonah would say all these things that are really offensive to me and I would ask him to stop all the time. I would constantly tell him he had to stop talking like that. We've been friends now ten years, and last year he came out to me. He called and said he went on a date with a guy, and I said, 'Oh, was he cute?' [Laughter erupts.] That was my response."

"Wait, so was he cute?!" John asks.

"Yes, actually he turned out to be very cute," says Etta.

"Ms. Swan, you are MARRIED!" Kimberly shouts.

"Oh my gosh," Etta says, feigning exasperation. "Anyway, it wasn't until about a week later that he called me and told me that he appreciated that I stand up for people even though he wasn't in a space where he could stand up for himself. So, your language might not reflect what you think, but nobody else knows that except for you. If somebody is in this classroom or if I were gay and you're using this language, it wouldn't feel very safe. Kesha, this could have happened to anybody; you didn't do anything wrong. Thank you for starting this conversation."

"Oh no, I support gay rights and everything, I really do. . . I probably should have used a different word," Kesha proclaims. "I can't believe you said he was cute, Ms. Swan!"

Etta's focus on safety in her response resonates with the language in the "Policy of Peace" her students sign the first day of class as well as with her own commitment to creating a protected place for students such as Carmen, described earlier. This does not mean, however, that Etta avoids conflicting opinions or shuns disagreement, as in the example with Phillip and the dispute over standing for the Pledge of Allegiance. Rather, Etta aspires to ensure that individual students and their identities are welcomed, even if disagreed upon—as long as that disagreement is respectful and does not reflect larger narratives of oppression. This is a delicate balance and one that Etta handles remarkably well, here choosing to explore Kesha's language instead of chastising her in front the class. She takes this as an opportunity to empathize with Kesha and discuss the phrase including its social meaning. Furthermore, her disruption comes from a place of love for her students and promotes collectivity. Etta illustrates for them how the issue is larger than one person or one word and is actually part of a social structure, of what she labels "a habit." She tells the class, "This could have happened to anybody." In this sense, she positions herself alongside her students, saying, in other words, "I also could have made this mistake."

And, there were times when Etta did make mistakes with language and her students calmly pointed those out, just as she did theirs:

"Ok guys, what do you think about the controversy of this being a genocide?" Etta asks after students have watched a piece of the film *Hotel*

*Rwanda* and learned the background information on the bloodshed in the 1990s.

"Ms. Swan, you just said 'guys,'" Tony calls out.

"Oh no! Thank you for that, Tony!" Etta exclaims. "What should I have said instead?"

"Ya'll . . . or team, like you usually do," Allison offered.

"Thank you, and thank you for holding me accountable. . . . So, what do you think?" Etta asked.

The students catch Etta's reference to the entire class through the normative masculine pronoun "guys." Etta's positioning of herself as someone who is capable of making mistakes detracts from students perceiving her as "expert," as the person in the class who bestows knowledge upon her students. This serves to shift power from the traditional manner in which it is embodied in typical classroom discourse (Cazden, 1986) where the teacher assumes the role of control and maintains a status of power above her students (McLaren, 2003). Not only does she disrupt language that reflects oppressive structures, but her students have learned to as well.

Etta's attention to authority and disrupting it is therefore another element that characterizes her transformative language practices (Grant & Agosto, 2008). Teachers' recognition of the majority power they possess in the classroom because they are likely the only adult figure present and being vigilant about how they use that power in both positive and negative ways (Cooper, 2003) is crucial. Although the very nature of schools places teachers in these positions, it is up to the educator to uncover and mediate that role. Etta's audible response to typical classroom discourse purposefully undermines dominant, accepted patterns, including her power as a teacher.

## Employing Symbolic Language

Discursive practices include more than verbal utterances. Other aspects, such as visible classroom materials, also exhibit transformative practices that are socially just. This extends Geneva Gay's (2002) idea of *symbolic curriculum*, which she explains as the "images, symbols, icons, mottoes, awards, celebrations, and other artifacts that are used to teach students knowledge, skills, morals, and values" (p. 108). The teacher's classroom is a "valuable 'advertising' space," (p. 108) and one from which students learn both from what is present and what is not. While Gay refers specifically to materials that convey ethnic and cultural diversity, I draw upon her notion here to include material that connotes social justice in any of its myriad forms.

In Etta's case, before even entering the room, her "Safe Zone" sticker on her door stands out, which is a visible signifier of her commitment to providing support for individuals who identify as LGBTQIA. It also denotes that she has participated in a training session at a university to receive this signage. Thus, by displaying the badge on her classroom door, Etta associates herself with the causes related to these populations and affirms herself as an advocate for students or staff who identify as LGBTQIA. Inside her classroom, the walls bear teacher-created posters and some that were produced professionally. One poster comprises two columns, one labeled "Yes" above a list of items that can be recycled, such as paper, aluminum, and glass, and another labeled "No" above a separate list of items such as cloth, wood, and food wrappers. An additional homemade poster reads, "Before you speak, think" and then lists beside each letter of "think" vertically: "T—Is it TRUE? H—Is it HELPFUL? I—Is it INSPIRING? N—Is it NECESSARY? K—Is it KIND?" These word–images exemplify Etta's commitment to caring for the environment and also exhibit her overall vow to maintain a constructive atmosphere for her students.

Beyond these posters, the nature of those that appear to be mass-produced are somewhat atypical for an English classroom, where quotes from famous authors and images of the Globe Theater are ubiquitous. Although generic in their immediate appearance, they express a political stance, one aligned with social justice. They include images that contain lists of words to serve as substitutes for offensive uses of the words "gay" and "retarded." One poster reads,

> That's so . . .
> Ridiculous
> Absurd
> Pointless
> Uncool
> Irrational
> Senseless
> Illogical
> Trivial
> Ill-considered
> Dull
> . . . and you choose
> Retarded?
> Buy a dictionary.

The alternative words are colorful and presented as a sort of Wordle, a visual cluster of words shaped somewhat like a cloud (www.wordle.net/create), with some bolded and more easily legible than others.

Finally, behind her desk, Etta has her own word image that she created. It states,

> Reasons why I <3 My Job:
> I get to help others

I get to learn new things and I'm encouraged to do so
I have friends here who support me
There are plenty of opportunities for growth
I am able to make my classroom a safe space
It allows me to advocate for students, especially those who are "othered"
It allows me to spend time with my husband

As symbolic curriculum, the message that this list conveys to students is undeniable—Etta loves them and the work she does as a teacher. This solitary piece echoes the practices already seen in Etta's classroom, including her attention to marginalized students, her desire to create safe spaces, and her propensity for personal growth. Finally, beside this poster is a bulletin board full of letters and cards from former students thanking Etta for her efforts or updating her on their lives. These serve to show that Etta values her students as individuals beyond her classroom and that she is recognized by others for her dedication to them.

The artifacts in Etta's classroom therefore promote environmental, social, political, and personal responsibility. Images and symbols correspond to the goals and attributes of Etta's broader transformative language pedagogies. She creates a shared environment in which her own language is inclusive of students and their perspectives but also in which she teaches students the importance of the language they choose and disrupts normalized usages that perpetuate persecution. As a whole, Etta maintains her moral commitment to equity and justice throughout this discourse and communicates her stance to those present in her class.

## PEDAGOGIC ADVICE: TRANSLATING TO TEACHING STRATEGIES

In this chapter, I analyze how one teacher works to develop relationships with her students, and I also examine her responses to injustices, exploring how she advocates for students who uphold nondominant positions in classroom instances with students as well as with colleagues in her building. Her language practices, which are essential to both building inclusive spaces and to interrupting taken-for-granted expressions that are oppressive, reveal an additional component of social justice teaching that is crucial. As a whole, these pedagogic practices demonstrate broadly how social justice occurs in particular moments in the classroom. These moments, many of which are unplanned and arise authentically in classroom discussions and activities, are nonetheless undergirded by the teacher's careful consideration of the values she espouses. Etta's self-reflection, her own commitment to equity, and her intentional valuing of students allow her to respond thoughtfully, sensitively, and in ways that promote equity as situations arise.

In order, then, to prepare to act for social justice in classrooms and to learn from Etta Swan, I offer the following pedagogic advice for teachers:

- Locate one of your interests and brainstorm how you can bring it into your classroom curriculum to make connections with students on critical topics such as privilege or oppression.
- Begin with one cause (e.g., bullying or heteronormativity) that you will support and research that topic; imagine how it will be relevant in a school situation and how you will advocate for the topic and the students to whom it relates.
- Make a list of inclusive language practices and begin to intentionally use them in your daily interactions.
- Determine how you will respond to offensive language when you hear it, and practice your responses with critical peers who can provide feedback.

# CHAPTER 4

# Social Justice and Students
## Embodying Critical Caring

Often in writing about teaching, the word *care* is used as an essential element, the key ingredient for effective practice. While care is important, there is a distinct kind of care that characterizes social justice practice and is relevant to English classrooms—critical care (Antrop-González & Jesús, 2006). In teaching that is socially just, a pedagogy of critical care is different from universalized notions of care. Theories of care that generalize to all populations of students (e.g., Noddings, 2005) tend to do so in ways that ignore race and societal inequity and therefore reflect systems of Whiteness. Scholars (Parsons, 2006; Patterson, Gordon, & Groves Price, 2008) have identified problematic notions of care that are institutionalized in education, noting their assumptions of political neutrality and reliance on individualism, whereby the teacher is a nurturer and the student is responsible for their own actions without regard for the student's social environment or the way systemic forces affect the student. Matias and Zembylas (2014) argue that teachers' avowal of caring may actually indicate pity or mask disgust for students, particularly those from marginalized racial populations. Expressions that communicate care, they posit, are "entrenched in Whiteness ideology" (Matias & Zembylas, 2014, p. 320) that allows speakers to normalize emotions as nonracial and neutral and to set boundaries between themselves and others. Instead of such broad-based manifestations of care, the type reflected in the practice of teachers who work for social justice involves paying keen attention to students' circumstances and acting accordingly.

Embodying critical caring means first calling into question the assumptions found within traditional definitions of care and recognizing that teachers' and students' race, class, and gender exist in the classroom space and that those aspects of identities are parts of larger cultural narratives that affect students' academic performance and behavior. Second, exhibiting critical caring means working explicitly toward goals for equity and dismantling oppression. It denotes an understanding of students' circumstances and the backgrounds from which they come while continuously pushing them toward success. While building relationships and using certain language practices, as discussed in Chapter 3, are strategies that teachers can adapt broadly to any range of students, critical caring is a pedagogy more specific to the students whom structures of inequity affect the most. Because critical caring applies to those students so often ignored or mistreated in schools, and because assuming this stance can be difficult for teachers who wish to maintain the universalized ethic of care, it warrants the full attention I undertake in this chapter.

Many teachers, entrenched in the "hegemonic whiteness" (Matias & Zembylas, 2014, p. 324) that governs educational institutions, struggle with finding the balance between understanding and pushing, wanting to show they care but not realizing how their reactions can be culturally influenced and may even serve to perpetuate inequity. It is thus crucial to discern how teachers can exhibit practices of supporting students and reacting appropriately to their behaviors in ways that hold students accountable but also foster success.

## UNDERSTANDING STUDENTS' BACKGROUNDS

The majority of students at James Middle, the school where Beverly Mitchell teaches, lead socially and emotionally taxing lives by most measures. Although not all of her students communicate to Beverly what is happening beyond events in her classroom, she nonetheless infers from what they do share in class or from what she hears from colleagues and adjusts her interactions with students based on this knowledge. Beverly attributes the many labels ascribed to her students for behavioral issues to various events in their backgrounds.

> I think if I were somewhere else I would assume you're doing this because you're being a jerk today, but a lot of times they're doing that because they didn't have breakfast or somebody beat up their mom or, like, messed up stuff that I couldn't even deal with at that age. And they'll tell you about it, so I just really try to build a relationship with them up front and be nice to them and respectful of them. . . .
>
> They're not being bad because they are bad kids. They are just misbehaving for some other reason, and I think I may not have noticed that if I were teaching at like one of those schools in Ridgeview [wealthier school district] or something like that. But I think that that's such a good lesson to learn.

Beverly's emphasis on the context, on all of the parts of a student's life outside of her classroom, as being a part of her understanding of students is key. She says she interacts with students based on what she knows of them, realizing that this may not seem "completely fair or consistent" but affirming that she thinks this is "more equitable." Treating students on an individual basis with the idea of equity in mind thus demonstrates that critical caring has to do with eliminating oppression, a system whereby students, often those of color, are penalized without regard for their circumstances.

In addition to understanding students' family and home circumstances, she also recognizes other externally imposed obstacles as explanations for some students' behavior. For example, she links dropout rates with middle school promotion procedures, feeling that the institution of the school does students a disservice by passing some to the next grade level when they have not mastered course material. Her perspective is that this system hurts students later in life. She declares:

> They get to high school and they drop out because they've never had to do anything to get it. Like, it's not really their fault completely because it's very awkward. It's completely ridiculous how they are always promoted. And then they get here and they have to pass a class and they're like what, pass a class?

Beverly refers here to the trend of social promotion, or advancing students to the next grade to satisfy their developmental and social stage despite not having mastered the content for the grade level (Frey, 2005). Social promotion is supposedly a remedy to student retention rates, an attempt to keep students in schools rather than pushing them out if they fail. Beverly, however, believes that promoting students who are not ready for content at a new grade level hinders their long-term success. It does not insist on academic success, which is an integral part of critical caring. She grasps why students would drop out, having been pushed along despite not knowing the same material as their peers. Her awareness of students' actions in light of this institutional aspect is powerful, as she frames students' behaviors as reactions to the structures that limit them.

## RESPONDING TO STUDENT BEHAVIOR

Critical caring, however, involves more than understanding. It includes channeling that cognizance into validation of the student, rather than offering youth only empty words or sympathy. Beverly's reactions to student eruptions include allowing students the time they require to recuperate or to process what they are feeling.

> Michael, an African American male student, enters the room quietly between bells as his classmates bustle in and take their seats. As Beverly begins instructing the class, he places his head on his desk. Students discuss in their table groups and Beverly circulates around the class. When she approaches Michael's desk, she leans over and asks, "Are you ok?"

Michael does not respond.

"Are you having a bad day?" she says in a low, concerned, tone.

Michael doesn't move.

"Ok, just do this, tell me that you're ok. Are you ok?"

Michael barely nods his head.

"Ok, you take the time you need right now," Beverly says and continues to the next group.

When the bell rings for class dismissal and Michael exits the room, Beverly walks beside him to the door and gently says, "You ok? All right, well, in tutoring on Wednesday we'll get you caught up, because you can't miss that work."

Michael nods.

Beverly knows that Michael is in transition between his father's home and another new house with different family members. He is, in fact, unsure with whom he will live permanently. Beverly shares her experience with situations such as this:

> I know when they are upset, I can tell. And most of the time they don't want to be bugged about it or forced to share what is wrong, and that's ok. I get that. If I can tell they are ok, as long as I know they are ok, I assure them they can talk to me if they want to, but otherwise I just leave them alone if that's what they want.

She also recognizes that football, which had been a solid outlet for Michael, has come to an end for the season. She thus allows his comportment in class and draws little attention to it other than to make him tell her that he is "ok." She makes it clear to him that she cares about his well-being first. At the same time, she refuses to let him miss a whole class period of work, acknowledging that this would put him behind his peers. She explains that this attitude is actually part of her school culture:

> I think that our school in general is concerned with issues of social justice. We do tutoring on Wednesdays for, you know, 2 or 3 hours, and it's not just volunteer, it's like you will be here and you will teach kids if they need help, or, I just think the whole like climate is kind of centered towards that.

Her reference to Michael's tutoring, then, is a time when she plans to account for the material he missed. Her caring allows him to process whatever he needs to in the moment, but it does not excuse him from schoolwork or prevent her from holding him accountable. Beverly knows that simply feeling sorry for students, or permitting them to "check out" on a consistent basis because of their circumstances, does little in the way of their success. In fact, Gay (2010) refers to such a response as "academic neglect" (p. 54) because "all attributes of caring must be translated into actions for them to be of much value in improving the achievement of culturally diverse students" (p. 53). By exempting students from learning, teachers can actually contribute to their cumulative disadvantage (Barry, 2005), further inhibiting them and thereby setting students up for failure as they progress through school.

While Michael illustrates a somewhat calm manifestation of a behavior issue, Beverly also experiences more challenging student behaviors that she similarly addresses.

> As the class returns from lunch, Brandon, an African American male student, comes in the room sobbing. Mr. Dack, the behavior support specialist, leans in the doorway and tells Mrs. Mitchell, "This should be a tardy."
>
> Brandon snaps his chair away from the desk and sits forcefully down, tears streaming down his face. He angrily mutters under his breath. Beverly sees him and asks if he wants to go down the hall. Brandon nods his head, and as he walks out of the room, she instructs the students to begin reading from the page number written on the board. She then walks with him out of the room, stopping at her neighbor's door to ask her colleague if he can look in on her students. Brandon and Beverly walk to a conference room down the hall and chat. She tells him, "It's ok. It's ok. Do you want to talk about it?"
>
> Brandon shakes his head, "No, but I'm not working with Mr. Dack anymore. I'm not doing it."
>
> "Ok, well when you feel better we can go back to the room." Brandon never shares with Beverly what is wrong, but as he works on regaining composure she talks to him instead. "Some days are hard, I know." After a few minutes, Beverly and Brandon return to the classroom.

Beverly's response to Brandon shows that rather than ignore or dismiss students' emotional distress, she searches for ways to assuage their trials. Teachers who operate from a stance of critical caring recognize that microaggressions, the "brief and commonplace daily verbal, behavioral, or environmental indignities, whether intentional or unintentional, that communicate hostile, derogatory, or negative slights and insults toward members of oppressed groups" (Nadal, 2008, p. 23), have serious effects on students. Microaggressions involve things like assuming, because a student is African American, he likes rap music or because she is Asian American, she is good at math. Teachers who illustrate critical caring, such as Beverly in these instances, know that consequences of microaggressions likely appear in their classrooms. They are sensitive, then, to student behaviors in light of this awareness. As a result, rather than superficial expressions of sympathy (Boler, 1999; Chouliaraki, 2010), they embody active compassion wherein they support students and consider their individual lives when they decide how to respond to them (Parsons, 2006).

Beverly connects Michael's behavior to external sources in the instance above, and, in the case of Brandon, she believes he has had some sort of altercation with Mr. Dack that spawned his behavior:

> I hate when the BST [Behavior Support Team] people who are supposed to control their behavior get them upset and then bring them to my class, and I'm like why would you do this? He's come so far. He used to steal and stuff, and I had his sister last year. And she's super, super intelligent but a total handful, and it took all year to work with her. And I don't know, he has been putting in a lot of effort. I just don't appreciate them upsetting him. If I'm going to upset him then I can deal with it, but I shouldn't have to deal with what they did to him. But that happens all the time.
>
> He [Brandon] was mad. Like he was like I'm not going in there, I'm not doing anything. And I was like, ok well, why don't you just take a little time. It's all about take a little time, figure it out. And then let me know.

What is notable about her response here is that she does not send Brandon out of class alone or away for the whole period to another room or to sit in the main office, rather she helps him to be able to return and learn with his peers. In determining feedback toward students, teachers personifying critical caring remember that all students, particularly students of color, must be held to high academic standards, recognizing that achievement is a key to gaining power in society.

Beverly's overt demeanor toward students also reveals her ability to consider the accumulating challenges in their lives. She may be shocked or saddened by their stories, but she does not pity her students. Parsons (2006) explains that within "culturally relevant caring," "caregivers receive without judgment the cared-for" (p. 26), which Beverly demonstrates. She learns all sorts of things about her students' lives that might dismay others. And although she may hear of "awful stuff and neglect and . . . we didn't have electricity for two months and stuff like that," Beverly applauds her students. "I'm like, Jesus Christ, I'm surprised you're here. You know? Like, good job." While she thus admits to being stunned by some of their stories, she enacts "engrossment," which Parsons (2006) describes in her theory of caring for students of color, wherein "caregivers receive black students by accepting the students' realities as their own" (p. 27). Beverly sympathizes with her students and maintains a level of quiet respect for them, which is evident in her interactions with them.

## MAINTAINING HIGH EXPECTATIONS

Beverly's knowledge that many of her students have experienced tragedies does not hinder her from also maintaining high expectations for them, an inherent component of critical caring. In her classroom, Beverly establishes firm routines, gives very clear directions, and expects students to follow them in order to achieve. One policy that Beverly maintains is her rule that students immediately report an uncompleted assignment that is heavily weighted in her class:

> The bellwork is on the board, and students enter class, take their seats, read the journal prompt, and begin working quietly. Written below the prompt are instructions to have the unit paper, a major assignment, out on students' desks. Beverly circulates to collect papers, and upon arriving at a student's desk who does not have the paper, directs the student to the telephone at the front of the room. A short line slowly forms at the phone, where students are calling their guardians to report not having the assignment in class. After speaking with their guardian, they record the name and phone number of the person with whom they spoke on a log by the phone. This is so, if needed, Beverly can follow up on the phone call.

This example speaks to Beverly's strong presence as well as to her clear communication to students of what she expects of them. None of the youth react negatively to making the phone call; they know ahead of time that this is her procedure. She establishes early on that if a major assignment is missing on the date it is due, students call their guardian from class to report their missing work. This keeps her interactions with guardians up to date and places the onus of responsibility on the student, holding them accountable on both fronts, the school and home, for their work.

In another instance, students are tasked over the course of one entire week with learning new types of folklore at a series of stations. Before they begin the project, Beverly shares a PowerPoint with specific directions for the activity. These include following the rules for work in stations, which she says are non-negotiable and if not followed will result in a zero on the assignment. In addition, she tells students to remain at their assigned stations for the entire class period, to ask for permission to get supplies, to keep their voices at a low level, to speak only to their group members, and not to disturb other students. Each station involves the creation of a product (sometimes as an individual, sometimes with a group), and the culmination of all five stations is graded as a major assessment grade. An activity at one of the stations involves students working on an iPad, which belongs to the school. During their turn at the iPad station, they research information about Blackbeard and locate images of him for their product design, which in this instance is a magazine cover.

Beverly believes her students can succeed with specific, transparent expectations that set them up for success. She does not assume they will know the "rules of the game," and then punish those who do not; rather, she directly communicates those guidelines up front. With this foundation,

she supposes they will be able to handle the week of completely student-centered learning and act appropriately each day. That she confers
the iPads on the students and gives them full access while she circulates
the room illustrates her confidence in their proper use of the devices. And,
the students recognize this faith. Abbie comments, "Most teachers probably wouldn't trust us with an iPad [laughing], but Mrs. Mitchell trusts
us, which I like." They thus sense that she regards them as capable adolescents. Beverly feels that

> Without structure and rules you actually do a disservice to the kids. Be-
> cause they don't learn anything . . . they can't learn anything because
> they're just crazy. I do think rules and respect are important.

As noted previously, Beverly's emphasis on respect goes both ways—she
believes in giving it and receiving it. In fact, she defines social justice in these
terms, stating, "Really I think that social justice is getting them to respect
each other and interact in a way that is reflective of the kind of society we
want to be in."

Beverly also maintains strict classroom policies throughout the year.
When a student eats in class, Beverly tells the student, "Ok, throw those
crackers away. Food in classrooms is against school rules." When students
are tardy, Beverly reminds them, "Sign-in. Remember you get detention after three tardies. If this is your third one, you need to show up." When the
bell rings to dismiss class, no one is allowed to leave the room until all students are seated and quiet. One student up and walking around can make
the entire class late in exiting for the next class.

Furthermore, Beverly issues directives in class in a manner that communicates her emphasis on student autonomy. She tells Jones, a student, at the
beginning of class one day, "I'm not going to hold your hand today. Get up
and go to your station and find out what you're supposed to do." At another time, she announces, "It's time to clean up. I'm not going to tell you how
to do that so figure it out." Beverly here epitomizes a "warm demander," a
term Vasquez (1988, p. 249) used to describe a teacher who pushes students
to develop self-discipline and does not lower her standards but is willing
to offer assistance to help students succeed. Delpit (2012) further explains,
"Warm demanders expect a great deal of their students, convince them of
their own brilliance, and help them to reach their potential in a disciplined
and structured environment" (p. 77). Beverly's language in these directives
indicates that she wants students to take initiative and responsibility for
themselves—not because she seeks "compliance," but because "high standards communicate respect" (Alexander, 2016).

Although these aspects of Beverly's class, such as her directives, may
seem overly rigid, her style reflects not only what is expected at her school,

but, consistent with being a warm demander, it illustrates what researchers have found to be effective practice of teachers of students of color. Cooper (2003) differentiates authoritative from authoritarian, noting that the former uses *"power for the student's good* [emphasis in original] and never as an end in itself or aggrandizement of the teacher's position" (p. 421). Beverly's intentionality, her thinking behind how she interacts with her students and why she does so, shows that she is not mindlessly commanding her classroom for no reason other than her own fulfillment.

Also, Beverly often enforces her directives with humor. In their report on ethics of culturally responsive teaching, Shevalier and McKenzie (2012) find that teachers use similar strategies to achieve their purposes. They write, "In the case of minor behavior issues, teachers used culturally appropriate humor, provided clear redirection, and moved on" (p. 1099). Thus, Beverly's wit exhibits a piece of her social justice practice of critical caring. She uses humor as an avenue to communicate her high expectations for students:

> Beverly openly addresses her students: "All right, sit down crazies," and they smile and nod as they take to their tables. One mumbles, "You love us, Mrs. Mitchell." One student, Nate, sits alone at a table (by his request) and often takes a while to begin his work. Beverly goes over to explain one of the stations to him in detail and then says, "All right? Knock it out." And after she walks away, Nate begins reading the short story to himself quietly. On the following day, she describes the next installment in the stations activity, but when she perceives Nate is not listening, she says in a good-natured, sarcastic tone, "Are you listening? Cause when you're listening you look at somebody." Nate nods in an exaggerated manner with a smile across his face. "Mrs. Mitchell," he asks, "can I use my phone to look up this stuff?" referring to the research requirement at his current station. "Yep, go ahead," Beverly responds.

Cooper (2003) also notes in her research on effective White teachers of Black students, "the teachers' use of an authoritative approach to discipline and classroom management was often accompanied by a firm, if not loud, and what to some ears might sound like unfriendly tone of voice" (p. 421). Beverly's sarcastic humor may sound as such, questionable to outsiders, but her style is a social justice practice. It is clear that she possesses and communicates clear expectations for behavior and that the students respond to her approach.

In addition to her expectations for behavior, Beverly also sets high goals for academic outcomes and truly trusts that her students can meet them. A chart posted on the cabinet door at the side of the classroom contains class averages on quizzes, which Beverly uses to motivate her students to earn better grades. Before one particular quiz,

Beverly points to the wall and tells students that the average on the prior quiz was a 90 percent. "Let's get an A this time," she says. "I know you all can."

"Yes we can," chants Brian. "Yes we can."

The class laughs and many nod, shuffling their materials as they prepare for the quiz.

Beverly's encouragement of students shows her faith in their capabilities for growth. Not only does she believe they can grow, but she also expects them to.

As a White teacher working with mostly students of color, Beverly must be ever aware of these expectations and how her background might influence her notions of care. She admits that at first she struggled with the type of care that is best for her students, and she notes that her firm style is the product of her personal growth between her first and second years of teaching. She shares:

> I have to be stricter and be willing to tell someone what to do rather than ask them. Which again, I think, is the way to have your class run smoothly and to have them, you know, do the things that they need to do in the time allotted.

Beverly learned that her previous, more relaxed methods of teaching and discourse patterns are not effective for the population with which she currently works. Eslinger (2013) contends, "an ongoing self-examination of how racism operates and how it benefits them—is crucial if White teachers are to work effectively with students from racialized minority groups" (p. 2). Beverly knows that Whiteness pervades her teaching, and as a person of privilege, she must constantly negotiate her background experiences with her students' experiences. She also knows that there are parameters to her expectations of students because of her race, and she understands those, stating, "I think it would be great if they had more teachers of color, and I think that the teachers of color can interact with students in a way that I'll just never be able to, and that's ok."

Furthermore, she recognizes that, as a White teacher of mostly African American youth, she must constantly reflect on why she employs the pedagogies that she does with attention to privilege and oppression. Part of the reason that Beverly maintains firm guidelines, she shares, is because she wants her students to become respected *and* respectful young people, independent learners, and productive members of society. Her practices of critical caring in her classroom demonstrate that she wishes to work against pedagogies that would either disregard students' circumstances or would care for them in ways that do not foster their success. Most important, she feels, is critically caring for students through methods that do not perpetuate color-blind racism and that do not hinder students' productive capabilities. Instead, she understands students and responds to them in ways that push for their expected success.

## PEDAGOGIC ADVICE: TRANSLATING TO TEACHING STRATEGIES

The practices from Beverly's repertoire that I analyze in this chapter demonstrate how teachers must be ever mindful of the ways they and their students are positioned by larger society. As a teacher, it is crucial to recognize how emotions, such as caring and love, can be colored by dominant ideologies that promote individualism and meritocracy. It is also imperative, especially when working with minoritized students, to discern the societal structures and systems of oppression that affect youth's lives holistically. Being mindful of both the self and the student can help a teacher conceptualize appropriate responses to student behavior. Setting high expectations for all students, but especially for students who are disadvantaged by dominant society, and taking action to help youth achieve academically are essential.

To prepare to act for social justice in their classrooms and to learn from Beverly Mitchell, I suggest the following pedagogic advice to teachers:

- Investigate your own sense of what care means and how you demonstrate that toward others, paying attention to the words you use and the actions you take when you express care.
- Create a set of expectations for student behavior and establish how you might adjust those based on student circumstances while also maintaining a balance with academic success.
- Generate sensitive methods you will utilize to get to know your students' lives and home environments.
- Brainstorm a list of techniques for communicating with students' guardians frequently.

# CHAPTER 5

# Social Justice and Curriculum
## Content with Critique

There is one essential element to social justice practice in English classrooms that has yet to be discussed: *content*. Stallworth, Gibbons, and Fauber (2006) remind us: "Although literature is only one strand of the English language arts curriculum, it is at the heart of everything English language arts teachers do in the classroom" (p. 478). Other disciplines tend to have structured material that is widely accepted and infrequently debated; algebra, for instance, follows a linear sequence that is not generally contested by teachers and parents. English curriculum, however, has for years been a space that has sparked intense controversy. The age-old debate over the canon, whose voices it privileges, and the need to expand or even demolish the traditional body of texts used in our classrooms rages on in the field. While some argue that students should be exposed to a cohesive body of literature to give them a common base and a resource to draw upon when communicating in society (Friese, Alvermann, Parkes, & Rezak, 2008), others feel that students should engage with literature reflective of their own subjectivities (Landt, 2006), and still others argue that students should be challenged to be explicitly critical and to name Whiteness through textual study (Glazier & Seo, 2005; Schieble, 2012).

The first steps to approaching content for social justice are determining what student populations are represented in a teacher's classes and what texts can speak to those students. The next move is determining what works can be used that inherently promote critique or that, when paired with traditional works, solicit critical perspectives from students (Dyches & Boyd, 2017). Thus, it is not only text selection that promotes social justice; the accompanying pedagogies are also important. Mere inclusion of multicultural texts does not fully achieve social justice—exposure does not equal critique (Banks, 2010; Glazier & Seo, 2005). It is the treatment of content that is key. Furthermore, teachers can also use literature that is already mandated by local or state entities to advance social justice perspectives—it is absolutely possible to meet standards through a justice-centered curriculum (Dover, 2015). Tate, Etta, and Beverly all elucidate practices in which they use literature and informational texts for social justice purposes, meshing English curriculum—even that which is required by their districts—with their equity-oriented frameworks. The three teachers employ pieces that reflect their students, use works that are fundamentally critical, and harness traditional texts for their own purposeful pedagogies.

## TEXT SELECTION: CHOOSING WITH INTENTION

There are many dynamics that affect teachers' text selection, including those imposed externally by district and state mandates as well as those experienced internally through teachers' individual preferences. The Common Core State Standards have impacted teacher choice to a significant degree. A list of Exemplar Texts, commonly referred to as "Appendix B," accompanies the state standards, and although it is meant to be a list of suggested texts, many teachers feel they should include those catalogued on the list because they worry they will appear on assessments related to the standards (Georing & Connors, 2014). A study by Watkins and Ostenson (2015) found, in fact, that 51% of teachers surveyed were willing to substitute half of the texts they were currently teaching with for those in Appendix B. The Common Core State Standards particularly affect new teachers, who report feeling pressured to teach what is broadly approved (Darragh & Boyd, 2017). Despite such perceived mandates, teachers do often have a role in what material they bring in for classroom study, whether it is literature or informational texts.

Tate is the quintessential example of a teacher working to reflect her students in course content, to find material that engages them, and to foster a depth in connection to those works. Remember that part of Tate's definition of social justice education is providing students with "what they need," and she translates this into the books, articles, and stories that she chooses to use in her classroom:

> I specifically think about my students when I design the things that I'm going to be teaching them. Well because the thing is, and I mean, it's good to be like they're going to get so much out of this, but the other thing is I'm not going to have to deal with all of these issues if they LIKE this book. You know I don't have to be like, sit down, be quiet, do this, do this, do that if they are reading the book because they want to read the book. It makes my life easier; it makes their life better. It's just all around a win-win, so I always, when I try and plan my lessons, that's a huge thing. Are they going to get anything out of this, are they going to appreciate this, will this benefit them?

Tate recognizes that what is often perceived as misbehavior, such as students' talking or being out of their seats, might actually be disinterest. Her approach speaks to Donald Gallo's (2001) opinion that schools have created "an aliterate society in America," because they teach children the mechanics of reading in the primary grades and then compel them "during their teenage years to read literary works that most of them dislike so much that they have no desire whatsoever to continue those experiences into adulthood" (p. 34). As a way to combat potential aversion to reading, Tate seeks texts that will get her students to both read and enjoy reading. She tends to select texts with adolescent protagonists or with storylines in which characters struggle with pressures related to racial issues, as many of the youth in Tate's class are students of color.

For example, early in the school year, Tate, knowing she needed a book that was germane to her students' lives, chose *We Beat the Street* (Davis, Jenkins, & Hunt, 2005) for one of her classes. The novel traces the story of three African American men who make a pact in high school to attend college and then medical school. Raised in a low-income, urban area, the three characters focus on avoiding negative peer pressure and refuse to succumb to gang activity. Events in the novel catalogue the loving families of the three men, their encounters with racism in school, and the various obstacles they overcome on their quest.

Although the town of Newark, New Jersey, the setting of the novel Tate chooses, is unlike Harperville, the community in which Tate teaches, in some ways, it possesses similarities upon which many of the students can draw. Harperville is an urban area with, as described previously, a rich history of key events, including school desegregation, in the civil rights movement of the late 1950s and early 1960s. The emphasis on African American community in *We Beat the Street* and overcoming odds particularly as it relates to education is relevant in this context. Not only does Tate facilitate this comparison, but it also occurs naturally by the very substance of the book.

Some parts of the text are explicit about drug and gang activity, entities with which Tate's students profess experience. She describes:

> I have one student currently in juvenile detention. We take him his work. We are trying to get him back here, to the school. He had done multiple things gang related, like, drive-by shootings, robberies, drugs. The real stuff. Last year he was selling drugs and we didn't catch it. He's smart. He's street smart. . . . He has seven brothers and sisters. His mom doesn't have a job, and he's earning money for his family. It sucks. It's really sad. He's a good guy. He's so funny, I mean we had so much fun last year. He came to school last year. Mainly to sell drugs, but he came to school and did some work, and then this year, I mean over the summer, his whole life changed. Like he really got into it.

Knowing that drugs and gang activity are a reality for her students, Tate does not shy away from including those as topics in her classroom. In one instance, for example, she prepares students to read a scene that contains information about drugs:

> We are going to read a scene today that contains adult content. It talks about making a specific drug and describes how to take it. If you all can't handle this with maturity, we will stop reading the book right now. However, it's in the book and I think it's important to go over and it's part of these guys' lives. It's mature content, but I think we can be appropriate with it? All you need to do is listen.

Tate sets clear expectations for how the students should handle reading this portion, and once they finish the section, she praises them for responding fittingly. She does not censor the material or shy away from its contents; she addresses it as genuine in both its potential existence in her students' lives and in the lives of the authors, for whom the book was autobiographical. In this way, she provides material that is validating to those students whose lives it reflects. Tate is not promoting negative behavior by reading this chapter in the text, as opponents could argue (e.g., Gurdon, 2011); rather, she is providing her students a platform on which to build connections with characters based on their own circumstances. By including the novel in its entirety, Tate presents students with an authentic portrayal of the difficulty of growing up in an environment plagued by drugs and violence and wrought with systemic oppression.

Tate's text selection is based on knowledge of her students' lives that comes from her informal conversations with them, from their responses to journals and previous writing assignments, and from their discussions with peers in her classroom. Although she knows the novel will relate to them, she also engages her students in classroom activities in which she explicitly helps them consider for themselves the parallels between the reading and their lives. These intentional activities also prompt students to stay invested in reading.

> As an introduction to *We Beat the Street*, students participate in an activity called "Four Corners," in which students determine how they feel about a series of statements, choosing from options along a spectrum of Agree, Kinda Agree, Kinda Disagree, or Disagree. Tate labels each corner of her classroom with the corresponding word on a large poster. She reads a statement aloud and students position themselves in (or near, depending on how closely they align) the corner of the room that matches their opinion. They then are able to share with the class why they respond as such, each volunteering a testimony or belief. One statement is, "Someone's neighborhood can determine whether or not he/she succeeds in life," and another is, "I encourage my friends to make good choices."
>
> For the statement, "If someone grows up surrounded by violence, gangs, and drugs, it will be harder for them to succeed in life," Natalie, an African American female student, rushes to the Disagree corner. Tate asks her to state the reasoning for her stance. Natalie declares, "I disagree with

this because *alllll* these things are a part of my life and I am already successful. I'm here and I do good in school, and I haven't let them get me
down."

   "Ok," Tate says. "So even with the presence of bad stuff in your life, you
still achieve." Natalie nods emphatically.

   In this activity then, students disclose a great deal about themselves and
offer information that will later connect well with the text. Out of the 25
students in this class, approximately 98% are students of color. The students themselves articulate, as they read, the relevance of the book to them.
In fact, Marcus, an African American male student, says he feels the class
likes *We Beat the Street* (Davis, Jenkins, & Hunt, 2005) so much, "Probably
because of our skin color," and another student, Danielle, an African American female student, shares, "It just relates to us."

   Tate is unambiguous in wanting to show her students "real models of
people who look like them" who achieve their goals:

   These three doctors came from nothing and amounted to a lot. This is
   a big deal. I feel like 8th grade is that year for a lot of these kids, where
   they make—and I've seen it happen—where students make clear decisions about their future. One girl in particular that I'm thinking of just was
   hanging out with the wrong group and we've had three parent conferences this year just with her. Trying to, her mom knows it too, she told us
   this is the year, it's make it or break it right now and she's doing horribly.
   She's so smart though. But she just hangs out with the wrong people,
   and I just feel like they don't usually get that message. And I feel like it's
   always negative. Like you have to do this or you need to do this or you're
   not doing this. And they don't ever get like you CAN do this. . . . You are
   capable of doing this.

   Tate hopes the book can inspire her students and send them an encouraging message for their futures, both immediately and in the long
term. She extends the reflections of her students in curriculum through
her pedagogies of employing activities that inspire her students toward
their futures. A major project she assigns students alongside their study
of the novel is an "Occupation Project," in which Tate teams up with
the school counselor to help students discover their own personal qualities and potential careers that match those. Students conduct research on
three jobs to which they aspire, including examining how much education
is required to obtain the job, what types of skills are necessary, what the
work environment is like, and how much they will earn. They then select
one they can see themselves working toward in the future and write an
argumentative essay about why this would be a good occupation for them.
Tate notes:

In the back of their minds they are going to be thinking, ok these guys decided in middle school they were going to be doctors. And that's where
they are now. So, I'm trying to prove to them that you can honestly do anything from this point. You're in school, your future is still ahead of you. . . .
There are opportunities available.

It's a great way to get the students thinking about their future and for
them to start planning and creating realistic goals for themselves. The engagement is super high because they love to think about themselves but
also because it's realistic and applicable to their daily lives.

Tate, therefore, chooses *We Beat the Street* because it both relates to the
students in the moment and potentially affects their futures as well. She is
adamant in offering her students positive narratives to which they can subscribe, but she also goes beyond the text with pedagogies that help students
analytically consume the text and use it as a springboard for their own lives.

## Making the Parameters Work: Standards and Social Justice

As Beverly's practices of critical caring exemplified, teaching for social justice does not avoid, in any way, the rigor with which teachers should approach their classrooms. "We don't do social justice," as renowned English
educator Linda Christensen states, "at the expense of students' gaining the
kind of skills that they need to be able to traverse the world" (Golden, 2008,
p. 60). While some think that social justice is about teachers celebrating
diversity, being nice, and making everybody feel good without attention to
curricular content, such a perspective actually creates a false separation between justice and knowledge (Cochran-Smith, Barnatt, Lahann, Shakman,
& Terrell, 2009). Rather, "attention to social critique and to improving
society motivates students and stimulates knowledge acquisition" (Cochran-Smith, Barnatt, et al., 2009, p. 636). Therefore, social justice can, in
many instances, be a catalyst for achieving the standards. In other instances,
addressing required criteria might be a by-product of equity related instruction. Regardless, the two are in no way mutually exclusive. Tate again serves
as a genuine model for how to harness curriculum in ways that both uphold
social justice *and* satisfy the standards to which she is held accountable.
How, though, does she do it?

Our district has a wiki site with pacing guides and lesson plans for unit-
based themes for each grade level. . . . They tell us what books to read or
they give us excerpts to read. They give us common assessments, which
we have to administer to our classes the last week of every quarter. . . . So,
I look at those, and I say, ok the most number of questions is four on "evaluate arguments" and "recognize what evidence is irrelevant." And then I
think, how can I integrate that into what I'm already doing, OR how can I

cover that in a way, in a mini-lesson or with a book, that uses something that is relevant to students? I don't ignore the district stuff; I just try to find resources that are interesting. My big thing is thinking about what they will get, because this stuff is abstract.

The students remain at the center of Tate's practice, reflecting her definition of social justice, while she works within the system to satisfy its demands.

She goes on to describe other policies to which her administration expects her to adhere that involve common lesson planning and a requirement to submit weekly lesson plans created by her teaching team. Her 8th-grade Language Arts team meets and creates a set of plans collaboratively, according to district guidelines. They then, as obligated, submit those to their principal. Yet they find ways to work around this imposed uniformity:

> So, ok, we're all supposed to do the same lesson plan, but we don't really. We just submit one and sort of do what we want within the units. This is what we did last year too. And Kendra, one of our PLC [Professional Learning Community] people last year didn't even do the same units we did. But she was an excellent teacher. She had been here for 6 years. But we still submitted the same lesson plan. And I haven't had anybody come in my room and pull out my lesson plan and be like, "you're not following your plan."

Technically, then, Tate fulfills her responsibilities to the district in terms of the skills she teaches and the materials she creates. However, she does not do so at the expense of her equity-oriented goals. She continues to integrate resources and instructs her students in ways that align with her values. Tate ensures that her students become fluent in the concepts outlined in the standards and that they can succeed on the accompanying assessments because she knows these measures are valuable outside of her classroom. For students to advance to the next grade level and to gain skills deemed valuable cultural capital (Bourdieu, 1986), such as dominant language patterns, Tate complies. However, she does so through material of her choosing and with pedagogies that best meet her students' needs.

> On paper I know that my test scores matter. So I'm really glad that I have this stuff and can make myself look good. Don't get me wrong—it really bothers me. Because what am I doing? Am I teaching to a test? That's the exact opposite of what I want to do as a teacher. It's super, super frustrating. I hate it. I hate that we have to take this stupid test in the first place. I hate that there is so much emphasis on this test in the first place. Like it really fundamentally bothers me. But I also know that this is just one of those things. And, if I cross my t's and dot my i's and I look that good on paper and I can represent in the meetings like that, they stay out of my classroom.

> When I say make myself look good, it's not about me. It means I can cover these things but I can do my own thing without them constantly being on my back all the time. I mean I can give my students what they actually need. . . . It's just a little surviving and subverting.

Tate's words here reflect an ethical quandary that often arises in teaching. The feeling of teaching to a standardized test, as Tate notes, does not match her educational purpose and creates some dissatisfaction with her career. Yet Tate mediates this problem by intentionally positioning herself as an educator who teaches in a way that affords for her students' success on the test as a byproduct of what they learned in her class. This is necessary to sustain both her position and her desire to continue teaching.

As she notes above, in her unit on persuasive speeches, she approaches the study from her own design. Prior to requiring her students to write, research, and deliver their own persuasive speeches, Tate incorporates an article (Murray, 2014) about the techniques of Dr. Martin Luther King Jr.'s famous "I Have a Dream" (1963) speech. However, she is unequivocal in her purpose of not using the speech in a superficial or repetitive manner and explicitly shares this with her students, affirming that

> "When I was in school we listened to the speech and we analyzed the text and almost everybody has done that [students nod as she speaks]. And it's really important, but I want to read an article about it and how perfect it was."
>
> Tate asks Molly to begin reading the article aloud. She then pauses after a few paragraphs to ask, "So how should you open your speech? What is 'the perfect occasion'?" [quoting the article].
>
> "It means talking to the people who are listening and saying why what you are going to say is important," Eldrin answers.
>
> "Yes, exactly. So when you start your speech, you'll want to tell us why you care about your topic and why you are bringing it to our attention. Popcorn, Molly," Tate says, and Molly calls on another student to read.

Their use of the popcorn reading strategy is an established classroom practice in which students read at minimum one sentence and maximum two paragraphs before "popcorning" to another student to read. Tate feels that it helps establish classroom community and keeps everyone engaged as they read.

> Tate interrupts the student reading. "Why does he repeat 100 years? What does the repetition of the phrase do?"
>
> "It makes his point that nothing has changed."
>
> "Good," affirms Tate, "and this was in 1963. You might argue that things still haven't changed today, or that that they have but not enough

[students nod]. What is the Emancipation Proclamation? You remember from social studies?"

Justin answers, "It was Lincoln's order to end slavery."

Here Tate uses the content of the article that students are reading to connect to possible topics for their own speeches as well as to acknowledge racism in the current context. This brief mention of a contemporary issue validates it as an area on which students might choose to focus in their work. Tate continues to analyze the style of the speech and to facilitate connections to critical topics:

"Ok, and what about sentence structure?" Tate asks.

"He uses some long ones and then a short one to make his point really clear. 'We cannot walk alone.' Like a fact. Everybody's got to do this together," Violet follows up.

"Yes!" Tate yells enthusiastically. "Think about that. His sentence structure, just a short, simple statement, really gets his message across. So sometimes you need complex sentences, but sometimes you can just use a subject and a verb simplistically to really drive home your message. He wants White people and Black people to work together; he says our destinies are tied together, but he says it with those few words. It's really powerful."

"He's saying that not all White people are bad, because some of them are, but some of them want the same things. Some," Deshawn adds.

"Yes . . . yes that's true," Tate says.

A conversation ensues about what Deshawn means by "some," and Tate continues to affirm the students' opinions and understandings. Tate thus includes an article *about* the speech, not the speech itself, as a way of instructing students on speeches. Here she demonstrates a way to use content written by and about a person of color in a manner that is integrated into her lesson plan and the standards and skills she is mandated to teach—speech writing and delivery. While her broader focus is on strategies in rhetoric and public speaking, she uses a text in which she thinks students will be interested and that is about a topic related to their lives to communicate that purpose.

Rather than instruct students on rhetorical tactics in a decontextualized manner, then, Tate finds a speech with which students are familiar and a topic to which they connect to examine those strategies and to provide potential topics for their own work. She relies on her knowledge of the standards to which she and her students are accountable to infuse her work with social justice while simultaneously meeting the goals that are imposed upon her.

**Working Within Constraints: Locating Resources**

Another aspect related to Tate's curriculum and her choice of content is *how* she works within a structure to secure relevant materials for her students that echo their individual positions. She provides here another example of how to work effectively for social justice within constraints. This is not easy, and in fact Tate says the "hardest part of my job is finding resources to use," because, as previously seen, she so strongly wishes to connect them to her students. Tate draws upon her social networks and relationships with colleagues to gain access to and fund classroom materials.

As leader of her Professional Learning Community for 8th-grade Language Arts at Ivy Middle, Tate has a great impact on the texts that the teachers utilize. She was ultimately responsible for choosing *A Raisin the Sun* (Hansberry, 1959) as a reading for the year because it connected to a local production of the play that Tate found and researched. She implored her principal early in the school year to support a field trip to the play and to fund transportation, promising that she would raise funds for tickets for students who needed monetary support. When this request was granted, Tate then had to figure out a way to actually gain access to the text for her students, since the work was not in their textbooks or in their school library. She located a free version of the play online and made copies.

Knowing they would see a production of the play, Tate felt, in addition to the inherent content of the story itself, would be a catalyst for students' wanting to read the work. And she was right:

> I was absent one day and I left them with station work to do about the play, and I left them excerpts of the play at each station and an activity. The sub didn't get them to do the work, they did it because the students liked the play. When we actually saw it, the play made it for them. They knew what was going on. We had talked about it; they knew the characters, they knew the conflicts.

Resources, however, for *all* classes in the 8th grade are difficult to obtain. As Tate alluded to, the district provides units and lesson plans and suggests texts for use in those units. This presents an equity issue, but one that Tate again finds a way to work around.

> But then we don't have them available at our school or library. So for example we're working on the unit with the essential question: "What Does It Mean to Belong?" And I think one suggested text was *The Giver* or *The Outsiders* or something, and we didn't have any of those books. . . . So, I went on a journey to find some. I borrowed them from Green Middle. . . . They were able to give me 72 copies. . . . I had to hunt down, I emailed a

bunch of different instructional facilitators through the district. And no-body ever got back to me. Then I had to email all the media specialists. It was absolutely insane. That's only because I wanted to read *The Out-siders,* because I knew my students would like it and it would be good for them. I would never just go through there and be like, "oh no it tells us we have to do this. . . ."

Tate reveals here that while it may appear that she was solely working within district mandates— attempting to teach a text because it was ap-proved—she feels she has plenty of power in what materials she uses with students and she is satisfying both the mandates and her own goals. She is willing to put forth effort to acquire those resources in order to meet her students' needs.

In another instance, Tate submits a request for funds for a set of Scho-lastic magazines through the school finance officer with whom Tate feels she had a close bond. This person takes Tate's request to the school budget meeting and is able to gain approval. Tate recognizes her own strength in acquiring materials for her students, avowing, "I play this game like no other. When it comes down to it, this is all politics and it's all a game, and you just gotta know how to play the game." Tate definitely seems to be a "winner" at the "game" of pursuing supplies. Tate even borrows the copies of *We Beat the Street* (Davis, Jenkins, & Hunt, 2005) from a teacher who lives 2 hours away.

The kids loved *The Outsiders,* and this book [*We Beat the Street*] is kind of the same. The teacher had been a colleague at Ivy Middle and relocated that school year. I just got lucky that Melanie was like, "this book was great, do you want to borrow them?", and I was like, "oh my gosh yeah." She was here last year and we used to work together and have stayed in touch, so she knew what I would want and would be good for our kids.

Despite the challenges with which Tate is faced in finding materials, she does not seem to allow this to stop her from seeking content and using curriculum that she aspires to include, materials that fulfill her social justice purposes of reflecting her students' positionalities and meeting their aca-demic needs. She simultaneously finds ways to work within the system and to address the requirements of her state and school. She shows how locating individuals within the school who have access to funding as well as drawing upon colleagues outside of the school who have resources can be helpful. Bringing in material from online resources, as Tate does with her article on Martin Luther King's speech (Murray, 2014), can also be fodder for class-rooms that serves to relate to students, reflect critical content (Dyches & Boyd, 2017), and therefore achieve justice-oriented goals.

## TRADITIONAL CONTENT: THE PRACTICE OF CRITIQUE

While Tate's purposeful use of texts to engage her students and reflect their interests and subjectivities is a first step in achieving social justice through curriculum, really *any text* can be read in ways that promote equity and dismantle oppression. Both canonical works and multicultural texts must be read in ways that prompt critical reading and connection to the contemporary context.

This type of work, the reading of a text critically for implications of power and societal injustice, is *critical literacy,* and as previously described, it is the overarching approach of the English teacher committed to social justice. Wallowitz (2008) explains, "critical literacy interrogates texts in order to identify and challenge social constructs, ideologies, underlying assumptions, and the power structures that intentionally and unintentionally perpetuate social inequalities and injustices" (p. 2). Any text then, literary works that are part of the established canon, those that are less widely circulated, young adult literature, and newspaper articles, for example, should all be investigated in the social justice–driven English classroom.

### Exercising Critical Literacies with Traditional Content

Etta acts as an excellent model for enacting critical literacy with canonical texts. Etta's definition of social justice revolves around cultivating students as interrogators. Although she feels that her 9th-grade English pacing guide, provided by the district, is "not inherently designed for social justice," she instead uses the content for her sociocultural purposes, saying, "You have to sort of be the type of teacher who is asking those questions anyway." For instance, she says, "I tie it into *Romeo and Juliet* a lot."

> Reading Act 2, Scene 4, aloud, students make their way through Mercutio and Romeo's verbal sparring following the balcony scene.
>
> Layla, playing Mercutio, reads: "Why, is not this better now than groaning for love? Now art thou sociable. Now art thou Romeo. Now art thou what thou art—by art as well as by nature, for this driveling love is like a great natural that runs lolling up and down to hide his bauble in a hole."
>
> Etta stops Layla. "Ok, now let's look at this. Now that Romeo and Mercutio have been bantering back and forth with these sexual jokes, Mercutio says, 'ah, there you are. Now you are sociable, now you are back, my friend, my man.' Why is this what it means to be sociable—why is it that Romeo goes from being this eloquent speaker to all the sudden saying these jokes that are potentially hurtful, calling his friend a fat goose and making all these sexual references? Why does that mean being a man?"
>
> "That's just what guys do, they joke around like that," retorts Noah.

"Um, yeah, and they joke with each other about having sex with girls, but that doesn't make it ok," Adeline follows.

"Would you say this is a stereotype of guys?" Etta asks. Some students shake their heads while others stare without responding.

"Well yeah, it's a stereotype that guys joke about sex," Noah says.

The conversation continues as Etta pushes her students to consider how such stereotypes are "dangerous" and promote disrespect toward women. She asks them to reflect on society's gender expectations and masculinity and how Romeo and Mercutio mirror them in their banter. While a small example of how content can be approached through critical lenses (Appleman, 2015), Etta feels that these moments exist every day in her classroom.

> It's there. It's always there [referring to social justice]. It may not be as explicit in 9th-grade English as it is in 10th grade, because I feel like the World Lit curriculum has the human rights unit and has other units that let us examine and compare our culture to others. So you might have to get creative, but there are always ways, there are always connections to things like race, class, and gender—to binaries and privileges. And I try to help my students see and question them and apply them to their own lives.

At other moments during their reading, Etta specifically focuses on female gender roles. She asks, for instance, about Juliet's parents' expectations for her: "Even though many women in the U.S. today don't necessarily have an arranged marriage like Juliet's with Paris, how are women's choices limited in our culture?" Through her questioning practices, she demonstrates Kumashiro's (2004) point: "The 'classics' are not inherently oppressive: They can be useful in an anti-oppressive lesson if teachers ask questions about the ways they reinforce the privilege of only certain experiences and perspectives" (p. 75). In her exploration of gender in Shakespeare's play, Etta helps her students discern whose experiences the text privileges, how, and whose collective story it espouses. All are social justice practices of critical literacy—of reading a text to analyze for power and oppression.

This treatment of canonical texts extends into Etta's sophomore World Literature curriculum as well. The books in this course, perhaps not surprisingly, include a study of the Holocaust, mainly through Elie Wiesel's (1955) *Night* and Markus Zusak's (2005) *The Book Thief*. Literature related to that event is now typically included in such sequences, and this is reflected in the district's provided pacing guide that includes the topic and indicates the major works Etta is to use for the unit. What is striking, however, are the connections she then draws between this material and the supplementary items she selects for study, and the ways she engages students with both types of texts.

After students finish reading *Night*, for instance, Etta begins a series of lessons on the historic genocide in Rwanda. She discloses to her current students that her motivation for crafting this portion of the unit is due to sentiments shared by students in previous classes which assumed that mass killings are no longer possible in today's era. In this section of her teaching, Etta draws parallels between what happened in *Night* and the conflict between the Hutu and the Tutsi populations in Rwanda in 1994. They then spend class time viewing, discussing, and debating the film *Hotel Rwanda* (George, 2005) in its entirety, pausing at different points along the way (often at the students' prompting) to consider various related topics. In one instance when Etta pauses the film, she notes:

> "That line about genocide is really heavy and it's really important, historically speaking. For a long time no one in the government, no one in the Clinton administration, wanted to call this a genocide. They described it as a civil war. They said they didn't know the extent of what was happening. They had diplomats in Rwanda reporting to them, but there is speculation they ignored it. Then, they decided to say, which is reflected in this scene, that there were 'acts of genocide' happening. Why would they do that?"
>
> "I think they're scared to name it a genocide because then they'll have to help," Erin states.
>
> "Yeah, 800,000 people were killed in 100 days," Etta responds. "If we think back to our definition of genocide, does it count? . . . How was the Holocaust a genocide, and is this the same?"

The students go on to deliberate how the situation in Rwanda, does in fact, seem to fit their definition of genocide. One student asks, "How come we've never heard of this?" and others speculate the reasons why it might be that Rwanda did not garner national attention, spanning ideas from the United States' desire to "look good," to Clinton "not having a stomach for war." Their exploration of their own government and questioning motives for attending to human rights (or not) exemplifies notions of critical literacy. Not only are they discussing a social justice topic, but the way they explore it also reveals their depth of thought and attention to considering possibilities, which Etta guides them through.

> Etta reminds them: "Well, it's complicated. There were reports of it, but people in a lot of ways just didn't pick up on it and didn't pay attention. So it might not be all the government. But, some do think it was because we had just gotten out of Somalia, where we had gone on a peacekeeping mission that went bad. We lost a bunch of men and others got hurt. We didn't have a lot to gain from going to Rwanda. We didn't have a national interest. There are also potentially some racial undertones if you think about who we rush to help and who we don't. How does this idea of 'knowing' or of not knowing relate to the Holocaust?"

Again the students converse on American involvement and when and if we, as a country, act when we know atrocities are occurring abroad. They discuss the bystander effect, a notion they have already contemplated in their reading of *Night,* but this time in regard to Rwanda. They also, however, consider that often people do not intervene in situations like this because they are afraid for their own lives. "We were the heroes in *Night,* we're not in Rwanda. That's why we don't hear about it," Philip says quietly.

The *way* that Etta teaches traditional texts, exemplified here, is essential to reaching her social justice aims. She lights her students' paths toward becoming critically literate, or able to analyze texts for their inherent ideologies (Luke, 2000) and to dissect practices of articulation, meaning how a text represents certain ideas (Hall, 1997). Her students are led to interrogate American ideologies and our government's policies in foreign involvement. In reference to her students, she says she wants to "Get them to critique everything that they're seeing and critique the world around them and the decisions that are being made and the decisions that they make." For Etta, "everything her students are seeing" includes mainstream course content, such as *Romeo and Juliet* and *Night,* and thus she approaches it in ways that meet her social justice goals.

### Centering Dialogue

Etta facilitates her students' critical dispositions toward traditional content predominately through constant questioning that prompts them to wrestle with difficult moral and ethical dilemmas. In her Human Rights and Responsibilities unit, she continuously asks questions such as the following: What about people who have power and don't do anything? Who is supposed to look out for the human rights of the world? Whose job is it to look out for the rights of others? She allows students the space to grapple with these questions through large and small group tasks and discussions. She offers guidance but generally provides them the space to work with one another and reach conclusions together, which makes students feel accomplished. Although she asks them to think deeply and to search for cautionary resolutions, she always acknowledges the difficulty of the work, affirming, "Things are not just right or wrong, or set in stone; there is a lot of grey area—this stuff is complicated."

The dialogue in Etta's classroom is often a way to open students up to considering multiple perspectives on any one issue, regardless of the text from which it spawns. Scholars (Darder, 2012; Kincheloe, 2008) have explained dialogic teaching as a pedagogic style in which conversation between teachers and students as equals stimulates the consideration and acquisition of new knowledge. In this practice, students and teachers engage in meaningful discussions to build awareness, and through an open analysis of power, students uncover the way that those dynamics are present in local and global contexts. Etta often presents a range of opinions on a topic and asks students to "just listen" to one another instead of insisting on speaking only. Of this teaching performance, she says, "I'm not trying to change what's already there or change what's, you know, I'm just trying to open another door, like open another possibility. Like here's another way of thinking about this."

After viewing the film *Hotel Rwanda* and continuing to connect examples to *Night*, mass killings, and political ramifications, Etta pushes her students to consider what the limits are in terms of war and genocide, if in fact there are clear boundaries:

> Students have just read an informational text on the U.S. government's decision to drop atomic bombs on the cities Hiroshima and Nagasaki.
>
> Etta begins the conversation: "Could the bombings be considered a genocide?"
>
> Scott: "No, they were done for a reason, to make the point, to retaliate, for Pearl Harbor. It sent a message."
>
> "Ok, I'm hearing Scott say that the decision to bomb, where they bombed, was purposeful, and was done to make a point. But my question is, does that change whether or not it is genocide? Even if it's purposeful?" Etta pushes.
>
> "It doesn't seem fair to call it a genocide because the country was the target, not a group of people," Whit says.
>
> "Ok, we've got the claim that because it was not a specific race or a specific group of people then it's not genocide. Specific race. And that it wasn't done because they were Japanese, because this is who we were at war with at the time. Ok, so my thought on that is, and I am playing devil's advocate—know that. I am pushing on purpose. My thought is, does that not count as a group of people? Does that not count as a specific group of people? And then my second thought is—
>
> "—Japanese people live in Japan so the bomb was inevitably going to kill them," Emma interrupts.
>
> "Right, so in that, in that sense, is that not targeting a specific place, specific groups?" Etta retorts.
>
> "Well, no, there was nothing about the nature of the people, like their religion or ethnicity like in *Night* or *Hotel Rwanda*. It has to do with politics and government," Nick defends.

With regard to dialogic teaching with content, there are a number of interesting moves in this conversation. First, when Etta presses her students, she is transparent about her purposes, telling them that she is offering a different opinion for consideration intentionally. Interestingly, her students recognize her deliberate efforts to complicate their outlooks through dialogue. When later asked about her teacher's practices, Caroline, a White female student, states, "Mrs. Swan is always trying to get us fired up by telling us both sides to the argument and making us defend our opinions." The student reflects Etta's social justice goal of wanting youth to question and to think profoundly on controversial topics.

Also significant in this conversation is the shared power between Etta and her students, which is illustrated in their talk. There are instances, for example, where Etta is interrupted while sharing her thoughts, and the dialogue continues to flow as it might in a typical charged conversation. This contradicts traditional classroom structures in which the teacher holds the floor and students are allowed to speak in turn. That students are excited enough to talk at once indicates not only their involvement but also their feeling of discussing "with" their teacher. Tannen (2007) writes, "Overlapping talk can be cooperative and rapport-building rather than interruptive" (p. 94), as demonstrated in this conversation between the teacher and students. Furthermore, Etta's uptake and repetition (Tannen, 2007) of specific student points, such as the reference to "specific race," exemplifies her efforts to validate students' opinions in the dialogue and to use their words to build upon for classroom learning.

Etta's embodiment of dialogic teaching is thus apparent. Freire (1970) explains that dialogue "requires an intense faith in humankind, faith in their power to make and remake, to create and re-create, faith in their vocation to be more fully human" (p. 90). It involves having the power to name the world for oneself. This notion of dialogic teaching illustrates how teachers, such as Etta, can show this "faith" in their students. When educators allow for dialogue, it shows that they believe adolescents have something meaningful to say, and when they push students to further their thinking through dialogue, they avoid the banking model that Freire warns against, where knowledge is "deposited" into students' heads. Important to this conception of dialogue is mutual trust and an attitude of working alongside one another, where learning occurs "with" rather than done "for" or "to."

Finally, the incidents described here all center on a traditional text, *Night,* and show how it is possible to use canonical texts in the service of social justice teaching. Etta built her students' critical literacies from both a focus on the mandated text and on expansions of that text into others, employing the use of dialogue surrounding both. She was thus able to work from her district requirements to enhance her students' sociopolitical consciousness, finding the elements in the texts that allowed her to do so and building from them.

## SOCIAL JUSTICE CONTENT:
## USING MULTIMODALITY TO BUILD CRITICAL CONSCIOUSNESS

While the examples above demonstrate how to develop students' critical literacies with traditional content, teachers can also bring into their curriculum material for study that in itself is critical in nature—that prompts students' learning about social justice all on its own (Dyches & Boyd, 2017). The texts on which Etta, Tate, and Beverly rely as critical content are those that reflect notions of multiliteracies and multimodalities, meaning texts that reflect linguistic diversity and multiple forms of expression (New London Group, 1996). Their approaches to literacy, then, are far from traditional privileging of print texts and expand into the various formats that students encounter in their everyday environments.

Elements for the English classroom that are social justice related and multimodal in nature could be, for example, a news article on a current event such as #BlackLivesMatter, a Tweet from a famous actor, an image from a local newspaper highlighting controversial new building construction, a popular song, or a political cartoon. As previously illustrated, there are a number of ways that the teachers in this book engage their students' multiliteracies. Etta's reliance on Macklemore's music to examine social messages and her use of the website Rap Genius combines audio, print, and web-based modes. She involves students with the selection of their own musical preferences in a poetry project, again combining auditory, visual, and linguistic literacies. Tate's engagement of her students with a performance of *A Raisin in the Sun* and their analysis of it as a mode of communication reflects an example of learning about embodied literacies (Ehret & Hollett, 2014). Finally, Beverly's use of stations to teach folktales includes varied modes of presentation (e.g., through iPads) as well as production (e.g., students creating magazine covers). To further elucidate how these teachers illustrate multimodality in terms of content in their classrooms, I differentiate between their own presentations of material and those products that they have their students design, hoping to show how both are necessary and how scaffolding students' analysis of multimodal texts can lead to the construction of their own and, ultimately, to the development of their critical consciousness.

### Presenting Multimodal Content

Beverly engages a host of multiliteracies in the service of equity and to provide for the perceived needs of her students. She reflects Sanders and Albers' (2010) notion that teachers working with technology can cultivate a "'new ethos,'" or "a shift in mindset about both the content they wanted to teach and the possible ways in which to communicate this critical perspective" (p.

12–13). Beverly imparts her ethos, her care for activism and inspiring her students, through the multimodality she takes up in her teaching.

One consistent thread in Beverly's teaching is the inclusion of an "Activist of the Month," in which she highlights a key political figure to whom she thinks her students can relate for their involvement with a social justice cause. For instance, she provides students with a news article on Malala Yousafzai, the young Pakistani woman who advocates for women's education and who was shot by the Taliban for speaking out. Beverly shows students video clips of interviews with Malala and magazine coverage of the girl and discusses how they present different depictions of the youth who is a hero to so many. In addition to the Activist of the Month, students learn about a current event every week that is also generally related to a social justice topic, such as the United States' reliance on the production of commodities in third world countries with deplorable working conditions or the prevalence of bullying amongst middle school youth. Students, such as Talia, report experiences like the following:

> I really like the whole "Article of the Week" thing. It helps me keep up to speed with what's going on since I'm not, I'm not the kind of person that sits around watching the news or reading a newspaper on a regular basis. Usually when I get the newspaper I go straight for the comics (laughing). . . . I like reading it better because then I can put my own perspective on it instead of just seeing what other people are saying.

Beverly often supplements the readings with related news clips and asks students to consider the various sources and presentations of the same topic; above, Talia explains her preference for reading rather than seeing the story.

When Beverly introduces another Activist of the Month, Nelson Mandela, she first points to the bulletin board in the front of the room, which displays a poster that reads, "It always seems impossible until it's done" and is surrounded by photographs of Nelson Mandela at various ages and in assorted clothing. She asks students what they already know about him, and some respond, "he was the first president of South Africa," and "he was in prison for a long time."

> "As further introduction I'm going to show you this clip," Beverly says as she turns off the lights and then plays a 3-minute biography of Mandela. The video contains audio of Mandela from interviews that overlays images of him. An additional voiceover reports that Nelson Mandela will be known as the peaceful freedom fighter of our time. When the video finishes, Beverly asks:
> "What did you learn about Mandela?"
> "He was a black man in power and that is a big deal," answers Steven.

"Absolutely. How did the images combined with his words affect you while you watched?" Beverly queries.

"It makes you feel like you were there when he gave those speeches, like I'm inspired," Katy remarks.

"And why do you think they made the video this way, rather than just telling you about him?" Beverly probes.

"Well because they want you to see him for who he was, to hear his actual words. It's much more powerful that way than just quoting him, than somebody else saying his words," Ronald offers.

Beverly's questions solicit students' analysis of the multiple modes in the clip they watched. She asks them to examine how meanings are made and distributed (Jewitt, 2008) and how they are done so in a way that makes them recognizable to a large audience (Sanders & Albers, 2010). Beverly's students note here the effect of hearing Mandela's words while seeing the images on-screen, revealing their multimodal capacities to see how different modes of communication are able to impart messages differently and to recognize that combinations of modes produce messages that are greater than the sum of their individual parts (Hull & Nelson, 2005). Beverly's inclusion of this text mirrors the way literacy exists in real life, where one form, such as print, is often accompanied by another, such as visual (Kalantzis & Cope, 2000). Through the combination of literacies, texts can express a narrative with multiple layers (Vasudevan, Rodriquez, Hibbert, Fernandez, & Park, 2014).

Beverly continues her introduction of Mandela by reading a children's book by Kadir Nelson (2013) and showing the students the pages on her document camera as she reads. Students examine the pictures in the book and stop to talk about what they see. One image contains a scene on a beach populated by White families. The image has vibrant colors and depicts warmth and sunshine. The page foregrounds a sign that reads,

*"The Divisional Council of the Cape / White Area / By Order Secretary."*

"What does this make you think about?" Beverly asks her students.

Rochelle raises her hand and says, "Segregation. When there were separate areas, like bathrooms and restaurants and water fountains and stuff for White and Black people."

. . . The next page relates to Mandela's organizations of rallies to fight apartheid.

"Amandla! he shouted. Ngawethu! they responded. Power to the people!" Beverly reads aloud.

"This was Mandela's slogan, and it was in a call and response format. So he would shout, 'Power,' and the people would respond 'to us!'" Beverly explained.

"It's like during civil rights here," Ronda adds.

"Exactly," Beverly affirms.

Beverly finishes reading the book aloud, paying attention to a picture of the same beach in the book's introduction but this time with Black families on it, to represent the end of apartheid. She also notes the 27 years Mandela spent in prison as a result of his actions toward the cause. She then proceeds to show students the movie trailer for *Mandela: Long Walk to Freedom* (Thompson & Singh, 2013). Students are rapt with attention. When the clip finishes, Ronald, an African American male student, repeats the line "Freedom, it is an idea for which I am prepared to die" in a booming voice, mimicking Mandela's.

> "It's pretty powerful, right?" Beverly nods. "What did you learn from the video that wasn't in the book?"
>
> "The book left out how violent it was," Natalie states.
>
> "And why do you think that is?" Beverly asks.
>
> "Because it's a kids' book," Matt laughs.
>
> Beverly follows, "Do you think the movie trailer includes how violent it was?"
>
> "Yeah," Julia says. "There were those bombs and parts where he is arrested and you can just see the army hurting people and stuff."
>
> "Ok. Who do you think they are catering to? Who will go see this movie?"
>
> "I want to. Is it out?" Ronald asks.
>
> "And how did they make you want to see it? How are they appealing to you, Ronald—what kind of people would want to see this?" Beverly continues.

In this class period, students engage with multiple modes of text and consider the impact of the text as well as its design. In the first video, a more History Channel–sounding biography, students see and hear Mandela himself. In the second text, the children's book, students "read" the images with the print text, and in the third, the movie trailer, they view a modernized depiction of Mandela's story. For each of the three, Beverly asks about design, pushing the students to consider the impact of the creator's choices on them as learners (Kress & van Leeuwen, 2001). She highlights that the combination of the visual, audio, and musical elements of the trailer produce an appeal to an audience. Through Beverly's questions on the material, students' multiple literacies are engaged. Multimodal literacies pedagogies have as their goals "access and engagement of all learners" (Sanders & Albers, 2010, p. 21), as opposed to catering to students who might come to school already skilled in print literacies. For, as Vasudevan and Kerr (2016) note, students tend to have "multimodal engagements that regularly go unrecognized in classrooms" (p. 104). Multimodal instruction has the potential to reach students whose learning styles may vary from those to which school typically caters (Sanders & Albers, 2010), an assertion which Beverly here exemplifies through her use of three different types of text, none of which are considered canonical. Nonetheless, they are material she has added as critical content to achieve her purposes of teaching about activism.

Beverly's pedagogies include a host of additional examples and her students affirm her use of multimodal texts as successful for their learning. For example, she creates several of her own videos in a venture to "flip" her classroom, a pedagogical trend in which students learn material from media sources and then complete practice or work related to that material in class with individualized assistance from the teacher. The idea behind this strategy is that students receive the direct instruction that would be delivered in class at their own pace of understanding at home (e.g., they can rewind, listen multiple times, take notes) and then engage in the hands-on portion under the guidance and support of the educator, who serves as a facilitator rather than a static figure (Tucker, 2012). Intrigued by this method, Beverly took on the goal of working toward a flipped classroom and, in the summer prior to the school year, created more than 40 minutes of short videos on literary concepts such as *theme* and *dialect*. These are posted to her website and she directs students to them throughout the school year. She says that they are quite time-consuming to produce but that she finds them worth the effort. Her students reference these and share that they "like the videos she made herself that she shows us."

## Producing Multimodal Texts

The true focus, however, in multiliteracies and multimodal scholarship is on students—as designers and producers—rather than on teachers as presenters. Although exposure to diverse forms of texts and the cultivation of students' analysis of those arrangements is crucial, so too is their creation of assorted forms of texts that show insight and careful thought. Affirming "the increasingly multiplex ways by which people can make meaning in the world, both productively and receptively, can potentially represent a democratizing force whereby the views and values of more people than ever before can be incorporated into the ever-changing design of our world" (Hull & Nelson, 2005, p. 226). There is a transfer of power in allowing students to choose a mode of communication and to design the way they wish to formulate a response to a classroom inquiry. Providing such opportunities can "lower barriers to participation" (Vasudevan, Rodriquez, Hibbert, Fernandez, & Park, 2014, p. 547) and thus affords a space for students who

otherwise might not engage to do so. The tendency toward student engagement and inclusivity that multimodality affords, therefore, reflects the goals
of equity in social justice.

As a culminating activity in Etta's Human Rights and Responsibilities
unit, and after students have thoroughly considered genocide, war, and re-
taliation, Etta tasks her students with creating a multimodal representation
of what she labels "The Destructive Power of Hate." As Vasudevan and
Kerr (2016) encourage, Etta strives to "create assignments that do not privilege the word over other modes of representation" (p. 105) and thus allows
her students, in groups, to respond as they deem appropriate. For example,
one group

> Determines that each member will choose a word that is related to their
> readings and that communicates the destructive power of hate. The in-
> dividual members then create an accompanying image of the word. They
> decide to depict each of their words in German, focusing their response
> explicitly on their reading of *Night* and about the Holocaust. For their final
> product presentation, they stand in a line at the front of the room with a
> series of images and words written in their German translations, including
> "Genocide," "Death," and "Destruction."

The first group, then, not only responds to the task with visual images,
but their alteration of language through the words they call upon is a picto-
rial representation of the particular historical moment they represent. What
is noteworthy is the students' framing, a concept central to multimodality
that "defines the way in which elements of a visual composition operate together," (Sanders & Albers, 2010, p. 8). The words in German, for example,
are an interesting way for students to make explicit reference to the Holocaust. In making these choices collectively, they are then able to individually
determine how they want to depict the word they took from the group. Another group takes a similar approach and responds in a collection of visuals.

> This group does not use any written text in their product and utilizes var-
> ied mediums to produce three-dimensional objects. One is barbed wire
> wrapped around a piece of construction paper and another is a gavel they
> constructed using paper. Their inventions go beyond the Holocaust; the
> barbed wire represents the imprisonment of both Jewish people in the Ho-
> locaust as well as the Japanese in America, and the gavel symbolizes the
> loss of human rights as well as political involvement or lack thereof, as dis-
> cussed in the example of Rwanda. The detraction of humanity, they say, is
> a key consequence of the destructive power of hate.

This group relies entirely on visuals to communicate their response to
Etta's prompt. Instead of individual creations, however, they work together

to create two objects that represent one large message about the loss of humanity across history as a result of hate. Their project vividly reflects the broad themes they have wrestled with throughout the unit.

> Julien's group has fashioned a collage on a large poster board that includes three-dimensional elements. A stuffed goat represents the idea of the "scapegoat" across situations, such as the Jewish people and the Tutsi. Cans are included to represent the gas chambers in prison camps. Images of swastikas are drawn in several spots. Finally, three-dimensional bread and coffee stand out from the poster, meant to illustrate what the prisoners ate and drank and to show how starvation and death is a result of the destructive power of hate.

In this final group, members worked together to create one representation, although it contained varied parts. Theirs, similar to their peers' before them, applies to a wide variety of contexts studied in the unit and perhaps took on more literal than symbolic meanings.

By opening up the possibilities for responding to her question, "How does hate contain destructive power?" Etta allows her students "to use a range of media to tell a story when one medium is not sufficient" (Albers, Vasequez, & Harste, 2008, p. 7). Some focus more on an individual story—the Holocaust—while others tell, visually, a story of a broader narrative. Strategic placement of objects allows for this rendering. The project "supports a new set of literacy practices in which critical decision-making and reflection play a large role in the process of creating meaning, as well as a new set of social practices in which the viewing, analysis, design, and development using technology and the arts becomes commonplace" (Albers, Vasquez, & Harste, 2008, p. 12).

## CURRICULUM AND PEDAGOGY: INEXTRICABLE ENTITIES

There are various ways that English curriculum can become a vehicle for teaching for and about social justice. Content should reflect the subjectivities of our students, illustrating diversity in authors with regard to gender, social class, ethnicity, race, sexual orientation, and geographic location. Students have a right to read materials that relate to them in these ways. As Tate exemplifies, there is a range of sources from which to secure texts that accomplish this goal even when at first it may seem difficult or beyond customary boundaries. Activating relationships within the school or district with people who can provide materials and funds for texts are crucial. Working with colleagues to share texts and build repertories is also necessary.

Yet it is no secret that the canon persists in many school contexts. This is not to suggest that there is little value in works traditionally taught in secondary classrooms. In fact, the teachers in this book demonstrate that there is vast potential for working with canonical texts to incite critical conversations. Etta vividly illuminates how a common canonical text such as *Romeo and Juliet* can be a medium for discussion of equity-related topics. She also shows how *Night* can be a starting point for a study of a host of other texts that relate thematically but involve modes beyond print and stimulate critical dialogue on a number of vital topics. What an English teacher and her students do with a text can be just as powerful as the text itself.

Finally, social justice content in the classroom is not complete without multiple modes of texts because those are reflective of the world in which we live. These forms, however, are used in the service of meeting students' needs and not merely as reward or to solicit interest. By presenting students with material that is multimodal in form, such as the digital and visual media Beverly uses, and by having students create their own multimodal products, such as the text/image responses to an inquiry that students in Etta's classroom created, we see that critical content is just as necessary to facilitate students' awareness of social justice and to develop their critical consciousness.

## PEDAGOGIC ADVICE: TRANSLATING TO TEACHING STRATEGIES

The ways Etta, Beverly, and Tate use English content builds on the pedagogies discussed in Chapters 3 and 4. Truly, the distinction between content and pedagogy is at most artificial and at least fluid. While the teachers' broader pedagogies build relationships with students and promote the ethic of equity through their behaviors, their narrower text-related pedagogies work toward the same agenda. Most remarkable with specific regard to curriculum, however, is how the teachers operate within the confines of the district-provided standards, prescribed texts, and pacing guides to embody their values *about* students, believing they are capable individuals who can read and comment on their worlds, and to cultivate *in* their students their critical dispositions related to social justice topics. The teachers work within the system to find texts that speak to their students or to make the texts they do have connect in such a way that pushes students' critical understandings and faculties. Content is at the center and is the focal point, yet from it springs points of relation and disruption.

To prepare to act for social justice in their classrooms and to learn from Etta, Beverly, and Tate's content-based practices in this chapter, I advance the following pedagogic advice for teachers:

- Study the Common Core State Standards for English Language Arts ("Standards in your state," 2016, or the standards that govern ELA in your state) and create ways to work within those for social justice purposes.

- Choose a canonical work that you will likely teach, pinpoint the critical topic within it from which you can build, and develop a set of related texts that are multimodal in nature and educate readers/viewers on that social justice issue.
- Familiarize yourself with local, national, and global funding opportunities for teachers such as GoFundMe.com and Fundforteachers.org.
- Explore contemporary texts for your grade-level classroom that reflect your students' subjectivities and represent critical topics; a good place to start your search can be award lists such as the Michael L. Printz Award for Excellence in Young Adult Literature.

# Part III

# SOCIAL
# JUSTICE
# BEYOND THE WALLS
## OF THE
# ENGLISH CLASSROOM

# CHAPTER 6

# Cultivating Students as Agents of Change

## Social Justice as a Verb

In Part II, I described three teachers' social justice literacies with regard to how they engage students and how they strategically work with content. All of these practices are key to advancing equity in the classroom space. If teachers are truly to immerse themselves in social justice, however, they must challenge themselves as well as their students to act in the world outside of the school, to use their critical literacies to effect change (Cridland-Hughes, 2015). Social justice cannot be fully accomplished within the four walls of the classroom. Students, through performing deeds to better society, will "see themselves as actors in the world, not just things to be acted upon" (Peterson, 2007, p. 34). And, if they can establish such a self-image while in school, if teachers can scaffold them in this way, they are more likely to continue these practices once they graduate from English classrooms and become participants in our democracy. As Walker (2003) notes, therefore, "social justice is and must be a verb (about doing and acting) as well as a noun" (p. 185).

### MOVING BEYOND CRITIQUE AND THE
### POTENTIALLY DETRIMENTAL STATE OF HELPLESSNESS

If teachers allow youth to carry on in the world as it currently exists, they uphold the status quo and thereby perpetuate inequity (Gee, 1996). When, for instance, Etta calls attention to damaging discourse in her classroom, having students pause and explore the power of language when one student calls something "gay" pejoratively, she is planting seeds for students to go into the world and do the same—to engage in disrupting discourse. If educators permit such instances to go unchecked, they are complicit in these values. Being silent is not being neutral (Cochran-Smith, Barnatt, et al., 2009); rather, it is tacitly affirming the value systems undergirding negative words. Teachers, therefore, have an integral role to play in helping students learn, understand, and implement social action. If central parts of social justice

teaching are cultivating students' capacities for dissecting power relationships; examining current events, topics, and uncovering counter-histories;
and debunking normalizing discourses, we must also include teaching youth
how to act on the discoveries they make and with the skills they develop
during such intellectual exploration.

Educators, therefore, cannot simply teach students that there are hor-
rible things happening in our world without also engaging them in ways
to address those atrocities. In fact, one well-documented caution (Downey,
2005; Peterson, 2007) related to teaching for social justice is the tendency
for critical pedagogies to place students in a state of helplessness. Often,
antiracist, problem-posing, and culturally relevant teachings are effective
in teaching students how to *deconstruct* the world, but in practice they fall
short of helping students *reconstruct* those instances. Sometimes students
are overwhelmed with guilt, realizing the social privileges they possess and
not knowing how to mediate them (Bettez, 2011), and other times social
problems seem so big that they feel paralyzed to effect change (Sensoy &
DiAngelo, 2012). Downey (2005) avows that "to leave them in this state
would be irresponsible" (p. 37).

Teaching students to work toward transforming social conditions so
that they are not left in a state of paralysis, then, is necessary. However, such
pedagogies must be undertaken with care. Acting to break down discrimination does not mean that students will be able to completely dismantle a
system; to lead youth to believe this would be detrimental to their understandings of social justice. While the goal is for them to, for example, seek
ways to alleviate the afflictions of homelessness and to prevent its genesis
(Carey-Webb, 2001), teachers cannot lead students to think that they alone
can "cure" the issue. Youth disrupting racist and homophobic language is a
notable accomplishment, but they cannot be responsible for eradicating the
myriad ways that racism and heteronormativity are woven into the fabric
of society. Yet educators should want students to trust that they can make
change, to know that there is always work to be done and that the work
starts with individuals committed to a better world. Those systems will not
change without the agency of actors within them, which our students represent. Teachers thus need to strike a delicate balance in encouraging students
to take on the role of agents of change.

The challenge of achieving this balance, however, is that it is sometimes difficult to conceptualize and realize action with students, especially
as a novice teacher. After Etta's unit on Human Rights and Responsibilities,
which includes reading *Night,* watching *Hotel Rwanda,* and listening to
podcasts on NPR about the conflict in Syria, her students voice their feelings
of powerlessness to address such brutalities. One student sums up her mood
by saying, "There's nothing we can do, as kids," showing her lack of confidence in her ability to act and also her sense of futility given her age. This
comment comes directly after the students view a scene in *Hotel Rwanda*

(George, 2005) in which the dialogue between the hotel manager and a reporter makes a potent social commentary: People in the world watching the footage from Rwanda will do nothing except express superficial sympathy and then continue on in their own lives. Etta pauses the film after this conversation to engage her students in thinking about the message it expresses. She asks, "How do we get people to care?" and her students agree that it is difficult because most citizens today are desensitized to such issues, and while society might agree that current evils need attention, individuals will not respond unless they are immediately affected.

In a similar conversation in a different lesson related to Syria, Etta tells her students, "I'm interested to see what you think because to do nothing feels kind of crappy," and students brainstorm ideas for concrete action, including raising money and increasing awareness about unrest in Syria, but these do not morph into collective action. Etta broaches the subject of students as change agents, affirming their capacities, but a classwide effort or implementation of ideas for this goal to be realized does not form.

Etta admits her own struggle in this area:

> I don't know if I'm doing the right thing because I feel equally helpless and I'm telling them what they can do, and they can, but then am I setting up the tools for them to do these things? Or am I just saying yeah you can, here's some ideas. Or do I actually help them do those things? I don't know. And one of the things that I want to say is we can change the way you think about violence and the way that you think about talking about people.

Quite frequently, teachers believe they are being activists by virtue of the work they do in their classrooms—and they are not wrong. Etta is an example of one who feels very strongly that teaching is her activism. When she mentions changing the way her students think and talk, she is referencing her efforts to make the world better. Teaching diverse students to be critical consumers of their worlds, engaging them in constructive dialogue, and loving all of the students in their classrooms are certainly parts of teachers' activism. And, while Etta knows these are incredibly important, she also worries about whether she is extending social justice to the youth in her purview—if she is giving her students the skills they need and the abilities required to become activists themselves. She fears that suggesting ideas is not enough. Empowering her students, so that they too are working toward a more just world and critically engaging with issues of their concern, is the key.

In the case of Etta's classroom, struggling for action is not due to teacher or student apathy. The students are genuinely concerned for the well-being of others across the globe, and the more they learn, the more they sympathize with others in, for example, Syria. Yet because of the prodigious weight of the situation, they do not perceive any power to disrupt these events. As Bomer and Bomer (2001) write, "Perhaps for anyone, the idea of trying to do something to make the world a better place is scary at first. We all feel small and weak and ill informed; we are sure no one will listen" (p. 122). When the students express this inability, Etta immediately responds and assists students in thinking through options that include garnering financial support, voting wisely, and contacting elected officials. Because students do not attach to these ideas, however, Etta feels as though she has no definite way to get students directly involved with the cause.

Bomer and Bomer (2001) identify classroom instances such as these as "that awkward moment in the journey of social action" (p. 131) when students might feel "overwhelmed by the intricacies of the issue, or the danger involved in fighting it . . . or . . . genuinely ignorant or confused about what the next step is" (p. 131). Part of the students' feelings of inadequacy likely comes from the fact that they are thinking on a broad scale, in terms of what the country can do, because that has been much of the focus of class discussions. For example, as noted in the students' conversation in Chapter 5 about the United States' response to the Rwandan genocide, much of their attention focused on the United States' involvement in other countries' uprisings. It is thus possible that students are thinking about what the country can do, and whether it should intervene, rather than how they as individuals can do something, even if on a small scale.

It is therefore vital to not only teach our students to recognize inequities and to critique them, but also to lead them in acting upon these inequities so they can actually address the problems they identify. One tangible way to avoid a state of helplessness and to foster students' cautious hope is to incorporate social action projects with students. Through these undertakings, teachers can actually walk students through what it looks like to exercise their voices and to effect change.

## IMPLEMENTING SOCIAL ACTION PROJECTS

One method for guiding students to act on their worlds is through collaboratively designed and collectively implemented social action projects. This approach is exceptional in its engagement of students, relevance to their immediate lives, and inherent opportunities to scaffold learning. Different from service learning or volunteering endeavors, which each have their own educational benefits and limits, in social action projects, "students typically work cooperatively with other class members on initiatives they help to identify, plan, and direct" (Canadian Teachers' Federation, 2010, p. 1).

Students have "explained social action as disrupting injustice or collusion" (Young, 2009, p. 114). Thus, social action involves addressing events, people, or actions that students deem to be discriminatory or antidemocratic to attempt to affect the trajectory of those events, people, or actions.

This sort of work comes out of a classroom where the teacher has laid the groundwork for intellectual engagement with power and justice, where fostering students' critical literacies is a central component of routine pedagogies, and in which students expect to be challenged to analyze their local, national, and global communities. Students who have been taught to think critically about their worlds will also be more likely to think in terms of taking concrete action.

Etta, for example, routinely employs pedagogies, with both traditional and multimodal content, that facilitate her students' critical dispositions. Coffey (2015) describes social action–related instruction in the following way: "It is a philosophy that must be experienced, interrogated, and developed through everything from the curriculum you design, to the novels, films, and projects you assign to students. In other words, it is a philosophy that we must *live* each day with our students" (p. 7). Etta's assertion that she "can't turn it off" when she describes social justice is a reflection of how she embodies her critical disposition habitually. Furthermore, Tate's explanations of how she plans her curriculum so that it appeals to students, reflects them, and solicits their analysis serves as an example of intentionally organizing with social justice goals in mind. The constant considerations for justice in her lesson plans permeate her students' takeaways. One student, Kira, for instance, stated that she knew her teacher wanted the class to understand how racism could affect a person's trajectory through their reading of *We Beat the Street* because it was a constant part of their class discussions as they read.

Social action projects, which flow from the critical pedagogies illustrated by Etta, Beverly, and Tate, include creating, with students, a list of ills they wish to address. Students are most invested in action projects and more likely to pursue them despite roadblocks when they are working for causes that they have chosen. The problems that students identify and address can be located "within their school, community, and beyond. The goal is active citizenship" (Canadian Teachers' Federation, 2010, p. 1). Once students have generated a list, teachers guide them in selecting a project with topical clarity and viability for real change. Students then focus on one problem as a whole class or a series of issues in smaller groups and research those topics. Investigation into an issue takes many forms, including conducting archival research, interviewing local individuals, and learning from students' own experiences. Finally, students determine a series of action steps, create a plan for implementing those, and execute their design.

Because students choose the topic of the project and essentially complete the course of action it entails, teachers' practices during social action projects place an enormous responsibility on students and give them a substantial amount of power wholly unseen in traditional classrooms. Again, this type of teaching is characteristic of a classroom atmosphere in which youth are empowered *throughout* as agents of their own learning, where "critique must become a habit of the curriculum" (Bomer & Bomer, 2001, p. 106). Teachers honor student voice and center dialogue, much like Etta did in Chapter 3. Learners rise to this occasion when it is provided and show how much they are in fact capable of, given adequate trust and space. Students will certainly vary in their responses to issues and may have different paces at which they understand the topic under study. Young (2009), for instance, describes a class that decided to tackle homophobia. In the beginning of the venture, some students did not discern any problem with the phrase "that's so gay" (p. 110), yet through discussion with their peers and instruction from their teacher, they came to realize the expression "was not neutral at all" (p. 110). This incident shows that the teacher's role is crucial, and, rather than taking a hands-off approach during student-led social action projects, she should act as a guide to students in decision-making and in giving them the tools they need to productively institute a project. In addition, some students may be wary of taking on the responsibility of a project, which is where providing students options for action depending on their desired level of involvement is crucial. I will return to possibilities for action in a subsequent section.

There is therefore a great deal of negotiation in instituting social action projects with students. Teachers, as the traditional authority in the classroom, have the power to make decisions on how the work in their space operates. Their choices, however, when centered on social action projects, should be made for the sake of sharing some of that power with students, providing them with the autonomy to determine what their steps should be and how they will implement those steps (Bomer & Bomer, 2001). Striking such equilibrium requires constant attention from the teacher to determine what students need as they work and how to best *support*, not mandate, their efforts.

## Social Action Projects and Standards

Giving students the power to conduct social action projects need not neglect required parts of the curriculum, assessment, or standards (Coffey, 2015). Instead, the endeavor is the driving force through which to make curricular connections (Canadian Teachers' Federation, 2010). For instance, from Etta's unit on Human Rights and Responsibilities during which students read the required book *Night,* she could facilitate students' desired action to help Syrian refugees through having students research the topic in more depth, including historic and current reports on the uprisings and civil wars, and write government officials about the need to provide support. They could also raise awareness in the school and start a local campaign for funds and goods for refugees. Thus, with social action projects, reading, writing, speaking, and doing are central and are offshoots of the topic at hand.

Assessment of social action projects occurs throughout their duration, not just in relation to the final outcome. It involves ongoing feedback that examines how students plan and implement each step of their determined strategy. Assessment also includes providing students with reflective questions and self-evaluations such as "Did we acquire and use enough background knowledge for each task?" (Canadian Teachers' Federation, 2010, p. 5) and examining "whether they have worked hard enough to bring others together around their cause, whether they in fact have taken substantial action to bring about change" (Bomer & Bomer, 2001, p. 21). Teachers monitor students' progress along the way and evaluate the steps taken in terms of clarity and efficacy, while remembering the goal is not necessarily to overturn an entire structure, but to engender some sort of substantive result. Students produce a collection of evidence for these assessments, illustrations of how they planned and undertook action such as emails, calendars, notes from meetings and interviews, research briefs, or self and group reflections. The public nature of collective action often leads to enhanced participation, and these more authentic types of assessment have stronger outcomes for students. In my own experience, when students know they are writing or constructing a text for a real audience, such as publishing a newsletter for circulation in the school community or creating a research poster to share at a fair open to the public, they are more deeply invested and create better products.

There are several ties between action projects and multiple bodies of standards, including those proffered by the National Council of Teachers of English (NCTE), the International Reading Association (IRA), and the Common Core State Standards (CCSS). For instance, Standard 7 of the NCTE/IRA standards for the English Language Arts is to "conduct research on issues and interests by generating ideas and questions, and by posing problems" (National Council for Teachers of English & the International Reading Association, 2012) which echoes the very definition of a social action project wherein students research a problem of interest to them and about which they generate their own inquiries (Epstein, 2014). Furthermore, when students engage in action, as in Ladson-Billings' (2006) account of a group who channeled their frustration with drugs and crime in their community into a research project and presentation to their local city council, they prepare their work for a particular audience and fashion convincing arguments. This is reflective of Common Core anchor standards for writing, the 4th of which for Grades 9–10 is that students "produce clear and coherent writing in which the development, organization, and style are appropriate to task, purpose, and audience" (Common Core State Standards Initiative, 2010). When students create a presentation about a social action project for a governing body, keeping in mind their audience and selecting appropriate information to share, they are addressing this standard.

As an additional example, in researching the social cause they identify for an action project, students meet the 7th anchor standard for writing, which holds them accountable to "conduct short as well as more sustained research to answer a question (including a self-generated question) or solve a problem" (CCSS, 2010). These are merely illustrations of the ways in which action projects mesh well with the standards that predominately govern English teachers' instruction. Epstein (2014) encourages teachers to "identify relevant, pressing social problems that affect and interest the students and then craft opportunities for the students to meet the standards while addressing these social problems" (p. 15). Again, as with the literacy events that generate from the topic at hand, teachers can likewise shape occasions for meeting learning targets from the social issue.

## Possibilities for Engaging Students with Change:
## The Spectrum of Social Action

I have thus far posited social action as deeds students perform to address inequities they identify. Yet there are multiple types of endeavors that students can shoulder depending on the nature of the problem, their contexts, and the level of support they receive from the teacher, school, and community. The various types of action are also dependent on the environment in which the teacher works, her level of comfort, and the resources she has available to assist students.

Perhaps not surprisingly, social action projects related to English classrooms generally coalesce around literacy events, and these efforts are usually closely tied to indirect action. The Canadian Teachers' Federation (2010) posits a spectrum of social action in which indirect action, "influencing those who have power to effect change," resides on one side and direct action, "directly addressing a problem and effecting change," dwells on the other (p. 2). In the former, students might write to local governments to sway them to change or institute a policy, such as more in-depth training for police officers on implicit bias. Somewhere in the middle of the spectrum might be a project in which students raise awareness of particular topics through a school assembly, such as the youth in Epstein's (2009) study who advocate for a range of causes such as healthy eating, air pollution, and sex education. By fostering others' consciousness, these students were taking action. Many of the youth involved also proposed additional steps for others' actions to achieve their visions for a better world. On the other end of the spectrum, where direct action lives, could be students organizing a demonstration such as a walkout or starting a club at school for allies of LGBTQIA communities. From this position, students are physically participating in change.

Examples of students writing for social action include coalitions of students in Katherine Bomer's (2001) class who developed responses to the war in Iraq and circulated a petition against the war; others championed women's rights and sought to document discrepancies in gender representation at a nearby museum; and still others uncovered disparities in treatment by social classes in local neighborhoods and wrote to the mayor to voice their concerns. As the projects unfolded, Katherine crafted mini-lessons on topics that would inform her students' writing, such as incorporating statistics into persuasive writing or altering tone based on audience. Students' assigned homework was related to their specific project. Because their writing was meant to inform and inspire others to effect change, I categorize it as indirect action. This form of action provides an immediate, tangible way for students to identify their voice and gives them an avenue to be heard. Returning to the feeling of helplessness that Etta's students expressed and the potential for youth to feel there is little they can do, action through writing can raise consciousness and therefore empower and validate adolescents. Etta's students, shocked that they had not heard about the Rwandan genocide prior to her class, wished to bring more light to the situation in Syria and therefore could have benefitted from a letter-writing campaign in their school or local community.

Other possibilities for action that exist on the spectrum from indirect to direct involve students producing multimodal texts that transform how the public generally defines or discerns an issue. Inspired by Bomer and Bomer's (2001) work, Mancina (2005) channeled her students' frustrations with their community's negative image of their alternative school into a project in which they interviewed local stakeholders, wrote about their interview data, and created texts for selected audiences, such as a comic strip for the school website or a letter to the school superintendent that spoke back to the ways they felt they were stereotypically represented. Speaking back is a common thread in texts created as social action, and students appreciate the opportunity to speak back through visual and auditory mechanisms. Further demonstrating this type of action, Morrell and Duncan-Andrade (2005/2006) led a group of students through creating texts that informed the general public on issues they felt had been distorted in the public arena, such as "the media's interactions with and portrayals of urban youth of color" (p. 5). Results from their project included students writing for their high school paper, submitting to online publications, and presenting at national conferences "with the intent of providing socially-informed reporting" (p. 6). Their work was a counter to the dominant narrative, telling their side of the story about themselves.

Still other social action projects, such as Young's (2009) students' efforts to "challenge the silence surrounding homophobia" (p. 109) in their school, also involved multiliteracies as part of the process of taking action. For instance, students formed a Gay–Straight Alliance at their school, wrote requests for their principal to support a "Day of Solidarity" (p. 112), created posters to advertise the day, and constructed a school display "entitled

Solidarity and Awareness, which included facts and statistics about homophobia, names of famous LGBT people, definitions of key terms, resources for support, and other information" (p. 113). After some resistance
from parents, administrators, and teachers, a topic to which I will return
later in this chapter, the students were granted the day of awareness and
even led 100 middle school students through small-group conversations
about related topics. This project is closer to direct action, as students
conducted the day themselves and affected their student body. Direct action engages students intimately in the work of "being an activist" and
thus extends other forms of action such as writing letters or producing
multimodal texts. For example, Epstein (2014) describes a civic literacy
project in which elementary students "from de facto segregated schools
came together for multiple out-of-school meetings to build friendships and
an awareness of race and racism in society," concluding with a "video
public service announcement on school inequity and other issues related
to de facto segregation" (p. 2–3).

    I posit that these sorts of direct action projects involve a framework with
four steps: contextualizing, organizing, acting, and reflecting. This COAR
process walks students and teachers through each phase of direct action,
and the teacher scaffolds students' learning when needed. In the first step,
students locate the issue they want to address. Locating an issue involves
deeply examining the context in which it occurs. This phase comprises
extensive research on the history of the topic, its manifestations, related
legislation, and the key actors involved—supporters and opposers. Such
context-building helps students examine multiple viewpoints and thereby
enhances their critical literacies (Behrman, 2006) and their ability to understand the complexity of the topic. Historicizing the focus enables youth to
see how *systems* are often involved in maintaining oppression rather than
individuals or solitary acts. The second step in a direct action project is
for students, armed with the knowledge gained from contextualizing the
problem, to plan the actions needed to address the injustice they describe.
Planning and organizing encompass a realistic assessment of what can be
done, who it involves, and the steps needed to tackle the issue, from making
initial contacts to carrying out a vision for an event such as an informational
fair or a march. This phase is key to the overall success of the action and
is therefore a critical space for teachers' guidance and assistance. Here is
when educators can highlight gaps in research, direct students to resources,
or suggest revisions to action steps. The third phase then is taking the action, wherein students implement the strides they arranged. In this phase,
it is crucial that the teacher witnesses the action and collects any products
distributed so as to understand and assess the work in this stage. The fourth
and final segment centers on students' reflection on the process and, just as
important, their looking ahead. Youth can engage in reflection either orally
or in writing, and they can do so with groups or as individuals. This is the

time for students to evaluate the successes and challenges of their action and to consider what could have been done differently. It is also the phase in which they determine how they will continue to address this social issue, answering the question, what's next? Focusing on next steps illustrates that social change is an ongoing, often iterative process.

## Benefits and Cautions for Social Action

Engagement in social action, from indirect to direct, can have a prodigious impact on students' futures. As noted in the examples above, conventional literacies are ever present in civic engagement, and such endeavors furnish occasions for students to hone reading and writing skills as well as to gain proficiencies in researching, organizing, and planning. Beyond those traditional literacies, however, action projects also provide a platform for students to exercise their multimodal literacies. Youth learn to combine modes of communication to influence an audience, accessing the tools and resources required to accomplish their purposes, such as becoming adept on an Internet platform to increase others' knowledge of a topic. Finally, action projects also boost students' situated literacies (Gee, 2015), those skills vital to act within a particular context. For example, when students learn to justify their cause to a principal or to have a conversation about a critical topic with younger students, they learn how to negotiate themselves in and with positions of power—they assume an identity within each situation. These identities involve language, behavior, and a general mode of being. Thus, action projects affect students' identity formation, both in the process of implementing them, during which students learn new and viable positions, but also through the topics that students research and about which they become passionate. When teachers therefore craft assignments that allow students to physically create change, to act on their worlds, they are fashioning opportunities that can have lasting effects on the kind of person a student becomes, the interests the student follows, and the causes for which they may advocate in their own future.

    I mentioned previously that there is a delicate balance to be struck in approaching social action projects responsibly. The fourth step, reflecting and looking ahead, is so crucial in the model I offer for executing direct action projects because I am hesitant to push students toward "sound solutions" (Canadian Teachers' Federation, 2010, p. 6), or complete, packaged remedies. I worry that the term "solution" leads students to believe that there are simple fixes to social ills (Hytten & Warren, 2003). While I want students to effect change, I am not naïve enough to believe that they can completely eradicate many of the problems we should seek to address, nor do I want to foster simplicity in my students. Still, if we do not try, we perpetuate the system. What I seek, at the very least, are disruptions to systems, and if students are able to overthrow an unjust occurrence, then the best outcome has been achieved. I do not mean that we should not wish for the ultimate triumph, I only mean that we should exercise cautious optimism with our students and that we should incite consistent action toward a cause, a cycle that may never be fully completed.

I prefer to think of this work as coming from a place akin to "critical hope" (Duncan-Andrade, 2009), which as Coffey (2015) explains, "demands that we reconnect to the collective by struggling alongside one another, sharing in the victories *and* the pain" (p. 9). As the "enemy of hope-lessness," critical hope "demands a committed and active struggle," (p. 5) that is not built on false or simple hope but instead knows that the journey is long and may involve setbacks. Epstein (2009) issues a similar warning and resolve:

> A teacher might think twice about addressing relevant issues with marginalized youth, only to have them find that their voices may be silenced in the broader society, or even their next period class. I suggest that educators remain aware of this tension yet not become overwhelmed by it . . . teachers can prepare students to understand why their voices may be silenced while fostering their ability to see openings for their views and imagine how different their world could be. (pp. 65–66)

If we are to authentically engage students in social action, we must be honest about the challenges they may face and the types of change, however big or small or none at all, that might result. Youth will be engaging in the real world, whose only consistency is its unpredictability. To promise them anything otherwise would not create a genuine experience or foster the tools we hope they develop in these processes for social justice.

## CONSIDERING THE OBSTACLES TO SOCIAL ACTION

Etta, Beverly, and Tate all broach social action in their classrooms, but they undoubtedly struggle to find support for traveling outside of their individual classroom spaces and engaging students in their school or local communities to work for justice. Despite the benefits of social action that I outline, such work "is not systemically supported in American schools" (Epstein, 2014, p. 62). As revealed, Etta exhibits frustration in helping students move on their knowledge of the war in Syria, and she offers them websites where they can research options for action. She also talks with them often about bullying and is an advocate for a transgender student, Carmen, at the school, refusing to allow her students to speak ill of Carmen and encouraging them to do the same with their peers. Tate engages students in research and presentations that she titles "Occupation Projects" to help students plan for a future, with hopes that this will encourage them to see that they can achieve beyond many of their present circumstances. Finally, Beverly shows her students models of justice through her "Activist of the Month" effort. Exposing students to noteworthy figures who achieve social justice is a practice that is well established in the literature for inspiring students toward social action (Bomer & Bomer, 2001; Epstein, 2009). The potential to design change-agent projects is thus present in each of their classrooms, but perhaps not to the degree I theorize with COAR. What might be keeping these social justice teachers from fully pursuing social action?

## Resistance from Stakeholders

Etta is the most open about her social justice disposition despite pressures she sometimes feels from her students' parents or colleagues within her community. She rejects the myth of neutrality in education and embraces the idea that teaching and texts can never be value free (Appleman, 2015; Cochran-Smith, Shakman, et al., 2009). She realizes that she is "taking a stand" (Zeichner, 2009, p. 130) through her daily actions and words and by the literary and informational works and discussions she includes in her class. Despite the fact that much of the public believes schools should be committed to objectivity and present unbiased facts for student consumption, and notwithstanding the reality that teachers are often discouraged from making their commitments explicit (which is true in the southern part of the United States where Etta works), she nonetheless honors her purposes for teaching for social justice and welcomes varied critical perspectives in her work, even when she meets resistance.

One instance that Etta faced, for example, occurred when a student, William, relayed to her after class during the Human Rights and Responsibilities unit that his father did not like her because she is Middle Eastern and that his father disagreed with her teaching the class to consider events in Rwanda an example of genocide. William's father believed it was a civil war. Etta thanked William for sharing with her and reminded him that there remains to this day disagreement on the topic. Another student, Nick, in a separate instance, shared that his father was disgruntled over how Etta handled the incident in which Nick and Phillip clashed over Phillip's refusal to stand and join the class in the Pledge of Allegiance each day. Etta accepted these critiques and in both situations reminded her students that she welcomes discord and conversation about controversial issues in her classroom—regardless of whether opinions match her own. She models respect for others while standing her ground.

In addition, Etta faced challenges from her colleagues and wider community, particularly regarding her attempt to secure a Gay–Straight Alliance at her school. After having taught Carmen and having several students request the Alliance, Etta asked her administration for permission to sponsor the group. The former principal of the school consulted the district's central office, which acquiesced under the agreement that the club be titled a "Diversity Club." This, Etta felt, was not true to the purpose or original intent upon which the national organization was founded. She strongly expressed loyalty to the mission, charter, and specific goals of the alliance and refused to dilute it with this euphemism. Upon the assignment of a new principal to her school, she reintroduced the idea but then experienced delays in subtler ways. Although the School Improvement Plan for the year boasted the creation of a "Safe Zone Certified Staff," administrators did not take action toward this goal. When Etta approached them to inquire about steps toward training, it seemed that the principal wanted to offer stickers to teachers to place on their doors (like the one Etta had received in her university training) without legitimate certification. In terms of the alliance, Etta experienced ambiguity. She laments, "No one is saying no, but no one is saying yes, either," which results in her feeling powerless to move forward.

Thus, the threat of resistance from stakeholders such as parents, illustrated by the students' fathers who disagreed with Etta, and the potential roadblocks from individuals in the school bureaucracy such as Etta's principal, are likely reasons that teachers do not feel wholly comfortable incorporating social justice–related action into their classrooms. Etta's experiences with conflicts over her curriculum, controversial classroom incidents, and failed attempts to implement an alliance club for students demonstrate how a shared vision among key players can be difficult to achieve.

## Internalized Institutional Pressures

The fact that Etta maintains her commitment to social justice does not mean that she is immune to the pressures of the current climate of public schools in the United States, which poses challenges to the realization of critical teaching. Education has reached a time, as seen in Tate's case, when many district officials expect common lesson plans and assessments, and some even go so far as to design these for teachers or to mandate the use of prepackaged curriculum. Often these sorts of bundled curriculum do not include social justice topics or action projects. It is therefore difficult for teachers to feel as though they can work "off script" and allow students to direct classroom inquiries. Furthermore, some administrators expect standardized testing to be at the center of instruction, and the trend of linking students' test scores to teacher efficacy is on the rise (Henry et al., 2014). The attachment of student assessments to teachers' status of employment is therefore very real, especially for new teachers. Thus, "these seductively powerful forces lead many in the profession to opt out of engaging students in collaborative projects that take time and energy to produce" (Coffey, 2015, p. 6).

Etta, Beverly, and Tate all express fear and apprehension related to curricular mandates. When asked what, if anything, limited her social justice endeavors, Beverly replied, "The lack of trust for teachers that is increasing every year," which she felt manifested in her being regulated to teach through standards and text lists. Beverly truly believes she would "get fired" if she does exactly what she wants to do in terms of texts and activities. Etta was reprimanded early in her school year by the district curriculum specialist for including students' memoirs as nonfiction, which did not seem to fit in with the informational texts the administrator saw as nonfiction. Because of this incident, Etta exhibits marked anxiety when discussing how closely she follows, or does not follow, her district-provided pacing guide. Finally, although Tate "plays the game" and submits fabricated common lesson plans to her principal as described in Chapter 5, she does this out of fear of the consequences for acting otherwise. The teachers' warranted fears—and it is important to note that they are justified in their reservations—of backlash from governing institutions, then, hold a key role in how far outside of their classrooms they are willing to venture for social justice and action.

*Fears of Controversy.* Sentiments echoing Etta, Beverly, and Tate's apprehensions are common in discourse among preservice teachers. My teacher candidates often share with me their desire to enact social justice in their classrooms and to work with students on local or global dilemmas, coupled with an intense fear that they will be limited in that aspiration by parents, colleagues, community members, or administrators. The culture of the school where they will potentially work, they worry, will not be amenable to the types of texts they want to read, the discussions they want to have with students, or the projects in which they will seek to engage them. They anticipate that the controversial issues and scenes in some books or movies, for instance, with which they hope to involve students, will cause alarm. Their worries extend from the topic of suicide in the young adult literature text *Th1rteen R3asons Why* (Asher, 2011), to the rape scene in the now-established novel *The Kite Runner* (Hosseini, 2003), to having students write to a local official on a problem in their community that has garnered public disagreement. They wonder how they will answer when their future students question their political stances, distressed that revealing their personal opinions will in some way jeopardize their standings in their schools.

*Self-Censorship.* Some educators internalize this dread over repercussions for teaching about social justice and as a result engage in self-censorship. External censorship "occurs when published or shared works, like books, films, or artwork, are kept from public access by restriction or removal from libraries, museums, or other public venues" (Boyd & Bailey, 2009, p. 653). Self-censorship happens when teachers anticipate conflict arising from the study of a particular text or topic and thereby exclude it from their curriculum (Lent, 2016), feeling that "the status quo is safer" (Stallworth, Gibbons, & Fauber, 2006, p. 484). This type is less addressed in public arenas, including teacher preparation programs. Yet it is this indirect censorship that is quite possibly more prevalent in English teachers' work and is argu-ably more insidious, especially in the case of new teachers and especially as related to social justice.

Sometimes teachers censor themselves knowingly, choosing not to read a book like *Looking for Alaska* (Green, 2005) because of its presence on a banned book list or the fear that the explicit references to sexual acts will cause a clash with parents or the community. Teachers realize that parents wish to safeguard students from content such as profanity, racism, and death (Curry, 2001). In other instances, teachers may worry about administration or parents' concerns for age-based or grade-based appropriateness of mate-rial and thereby limit themselves. Other times self-censorship happens sub-consciously, such as when a teacher fails to recognize her own discomfort in talking about race as the reason she omits *The Color Purple* (Walker, 1982) from her curriculum. Sometimes, even when they assign a text with controversial material, teachers avoid it by focusing on more palatable ele-ments, such as the overall plot or specific character motivations. Centering these, for some educators, can help to stave off controversy among students and parents. Teachers might also feel ill equipped to tackle a difficult issue and thereby choose not to do so. In any instance, it is *the teacher* who has done the limiting. She has not provided students a potentially constructive, growth-filled opportunity to learn.

Self-censorship can affect both novice and veteran teachers alike: Veter-an teachers may want to avoid the energy it takes to deal with being ques-tioned, and novice teachers wish to escape making waves (Boyd & Bailey, 2009; Rickman, 2010). Because teachers often "feel isolated and power-less," without supportive administrators and colleagues, they "succumb to the pressure to retreat behind the shield of . . . books that are less controver-sial, but that may not compel the student to see another perspective or think on a deeper level" (Freedman & Johnson, 2000/2001, p. 357). Teachers can censor all sorts of texts, as both written and visual descriptions are equal-ly potentially inciting. When they eliminate either, however, they deprive students of valuable learning opportunities and spaces in which to become more literate critical consumers of texts of all forms (NCTE, 2004). Finally, teachers bear a tremendous moral burden when they self-censor (Freedman & Johnson, 2000/2001 p. 357); they limit their students' education, defeat-ing the reasons for teaching in the first place, in pursuit of their jobs. As an issue in social justice teaching and a reason why teachers may not engage in social action, fears related to self-censorship are worthy of close attention.

## Structure of Schools

A final reason that teachers may feel restricted in their capacity to create social change with students resides in the very nature of schools. Despite recent efforts to encourage teachers to work collaboratively and interdisciplinarily, we know that secondary schools are structured in ways that continue to encourage educators to work within disciplinary silos. High schools, for instance, are physically and metaphorically separated by subject area—students take courses in explicit disciplines and the school is usually geographically divided so that there is an "English hallway" or a "math wing." Furthermore, schools are governed by class periods and bells, which rigidly isolate courses into intervals of the day. When English is over, science begins, and the forms of writing that occur in the former space rarely occur in the latter. Composing a letter to local politicians, then, to boycott fishing where swimming occurs in the local community might mesh the two disciplines, but it would be challenging for both disciplinary teachers to work simultaneously with students to accomplish this goal in the current state of traditional schools. Finally, instruction in public schools is overwhelmingly expected to occur *inside the classroom*. Spatial boundaries make it difficult for teachers to conceptualize working with community officials or local resources unless those individuals come to the school, which largely negates the civic engagement element of social action projects. These institutional barriers therefore limit how students can work on integrated projects and restrict their capacity to work within fluid time frames.

Etta repeatedly mentions the lack of time for teachers to take on any additional responsibilities, such as participating in extra meetings or making more phone calls, in her context. On many occasions, she struggles to eat lunch between the required "Smart Lunch" tutoring sessions, which, in lieu of after school instruction, students with failing grades are required to attend for tutoring during their lunch hour. On days when she is not tutoring, Etta is frequently required to attend meetings that are held during lunch hour at her school. Tate coaches junior varsity basketball and is often occupied until late evening. During the day, as Beverly demonstrates, teachers are responsible for supervising the many students in their purview during class changes and at lunch. From their contexts, with so little time and so many limits, it is thus puzzling to them how they could coordinate social justice action projects and find time to reach out into their school and local communities. Although they have shown that they can accomplish social justice within their classrooms, they have a difficult time discerning how to move outward.

## NAVIGATING THE BARRIERS

Despite the immense challenges from outside of the classroom and the impediments that result from the inherent culture of school, social justice is absolutely possible and teachers can harness their critical perspectives to help students find ways to take action. It may be difficult at times, but it is nonetheless feasible—if teachers are adequately prepared to consider these obstacles ahead of time, have practice planning accordingly, and are equipped with the necessary tools for support. Anticipating challenges to social justice in advance and acknowledging the difficulties that might accompany the work is being realistic about the profession. While I wholeheartedly believe that teachers can and should be agents of change, I also believe in preparing them fully to make that change with not just the idealism it requires, but with the pragmatism as well. Albers, Vasquez, and Harste (2008) recognize these trials of social justice teaching as a tension "between the restrictive culture of political mandates, which values traditional approaches to literacy, and a culture of possibilities that engages and builds upon the new literacies that students bring with them to class daily" (p. 3). Learning to work within this tension and to overcome the hurdles described above is essential.

I identify several specific ways that teachers can begin to surmount the barriers such as those felt by Etta, Tate, and Beverly. First, social justice must be done in collaboration with colleagues, which requires that teachers assume control of their own professional spaces (Coffey, 2015) and establish allies who are like-minded. Many preservice teachers are concerned, when considering teaching from a social justice perspective, that they will be alone. Yet this is rarely the case. There are often colleagues across a school who believe in equity and teaching for social change, and with some investigation and an open ear, they can be easily located. Listen, for instance, in faculty meetings for colleagues who speak of students in additive rather than punitive ways. Engage in casual conversations in the hallways and at school events with peer teachers and ask what they are doing in their classes.

Most telling are the students themselves. Colleagues who also seek to work against oppression in their curriculum will have students read about controversial topics and discuss current events. Those student conversations will inevitably spill into English teachers' classrooms, or students will make connections between other coursework and theirs and share that with their teacher. Etta, for instance, when asking students to consider the rights of immigrants as human rights, learns that many of her students read in their history class the story of Jose Vargas, an award-winning journalist and undocumented immigrant who advocated for the DREAM Act, which proposed a pathway to permanent residency for undocumented minors. Knowing that the history teacher read this article with his class, Etta felt more confident to approach him as a potential ally in teaching about social justice issues and to plan a collaboration with him for the same unit in the following school year.

In another instance, Etta learned in a department meeting that a fellow English teacher also taught texts from the perspectives of critical literacy, requiring her students to look for the implications of power and privilege in their reading of the young adult novel *Monster* (Myers, 1999). This led Etta to ask if the teacher would join her in sponsoring the Gay–Straight Alliance.

Support for social justice pedagogies is necessary, and having someone who will also champion a particular text, project, or even cosponsor a club is indispensable and helps assuage the fears mentioned by Etta, Tate, and Beverly. Furthermore, soliciting the support of a department chair for selected texts is instrumental and gives a teacher a place to go for help if a challenge arises. Teachers can find ally–colleagues in English peers, an administrator, or an educator in another discipline area in the building.

Second, parent and community partners are also vital, because they can provide outlets and even financial support for action. Communication and transparency with parents is essential and, much like with colleagues, using this interaction to locate and then approach supporters will benefit social justice work. Giving parents the option to write a letter to the teacher at the beginning of the school year with anything they want the teacher to know about their child, family, or culture can generate relationships. It also provides helpful information about the family and their concerns and values, which can inform the teacher in terms of either the parents' support for social justice or their potential concerns related to a text or topic. Weekly emails about what students are reading and discussing in class is also a great way to initiate conversation. If guardians know what their students are talking about in class, they can further these critical conversations at home. Hosting nights at school for guardians to learn more about a particular theme or to engage in discussion with youth who are wrestling with difficult issues can also enhance these connections. Allying with parents and community members, and inviting them to also read the texts the teacher implements with students so that they can engage in conversations rather than extract pieces out of context to protest, is key.

Even when parents, such as the father of a student in Etta's class, might disagree, they appreciate transparency; knowing what is happening in their child's class, and being made aware that discrepant opinions are welcome and that conversations of all sides are considered and encouraged will often assuage their concerns (Hess, 2009). Stallworth, Gibbons, and Fauber (2006) suggest "asking parents to read along with their student as the class reads multicultural texts and inviting parents and other community members to open sessions organized around student-led book talks" to "provide ways of encouraging stakeholders' involvement" (p. 488). I have had wonderful experiences with parents who have read books with controversial themes along with their students. One parent even found *The Kite Runner* (Hosseini, 2003), which is  controversial because of a sexual assault scene, so engaging that she immediately ordered Hosseini's (2008) second novel, *A Thousand Splendid Suns,* which she and her daughter then also read together. This was not required for class, but the pair found the experience worthwhile and thus continued their reading relationship. My student frequently shared with the class related conversations she had with her mother and their growing collective understandings of Islamic culture and the Taliban's rule. In another instance, a parent liked *The House on Mango*

*Street* (Cisneros, 1991) so much that she bought additional copies for my class when she found out we were short several copies. Despite vignettes in the book that include domestic abuse and rape, this parent felt the coming-of-age story was so powerful that others should be able to access the text. In addition to parents and guardians, teachers can locate conglomerations of individuals in their community with whom to foster reciprocal relationships. For example, what organizations can students work with that will provide services, contributions, or guest speakers to the classroom? Building these partnerships and bringing people into the classroom begins the opportunities to move outward.

Third, teachers can use curricular mandates and required texts to their advantage, rather than viewing them as oppositional or limiting. Educators should find ways to connect traditional texts to issues of student interest that warrant action. Chapter 5 catalogs how a teacher can facilitate critique with canonical works, and designing social action is quite similar. If, for instance, *Romeo and Juliet* is a required text and a discussion of gender roles arises from a classroom study of the play, teachers can ask students where normative gender patterns exist in their school and community and how they can work to break these down to create safer spaces for all students. The key is to think creatively about how to subvert rather than expunge mandated curriculum. If the Common Core State Standards require a teacher to have students write "narratives to develop real or imagined experiences or events using effective technique, well-chosen details, and well-structured event sequences" (CCSS, 2010), ask students to write about their own oppression. If required to conduct research to address a problem, have students investigate a social problem of concern to them. The push for informational texts that is alarming some in the field (e.g., Moss, 2013; Schieble, 2014) is an excellent justification for reading about and discussing current events such as those related to the political climate in the United States.

Finally, teachers can rely heavily on the students themselves—incite them to action through textual study and curriculum and then let them plan and execute that action. When youth have an earnest desire to move, when they feel passionate about an issue, they can engage in opposition and critique in ways that only serve to better their literacy skills. The teacher becomes the support and not the driving force, a person to guide their action but not the originator. If students, based on their reading and discussion of the #BlackLivesMatter movement, want to organize a critical discussion on race for their community, then teachers can give them the time and space to do so as a classroom assignment. This addresses the above concerns of time and organizational constraints—if the students are leading the action, the teacher can continue her obligations of tutoring during lunch, for instance. Civic engagement becomes something she monitors during class time, overseeing what steps students have completed in their process, reading drafts of letters or editing materials that will be distributed. Rather than an added responsibility, something to be organized during planning or after school, the students are doing the arranging and the teacher facilitates the process, providing instruction as she sees fit.

## Embracing the Political

In addition to these recommendations for overcoming institutional concerns, I also advocate several others in relation to the aspect of fear and self-censorship. Most importantly, teachers must embrace the fact that education is never neutral and that all texts and classroom actions are already inherently ideological (Segall, 2004; Yoon, Simpson, & Haag, 2010). Every single decision a teacher makes is backed by some adherence to a political stance, and the sooner she realizes that the better equipped she will be to respond to claims for objectivity and neutrality in education. If Etta had chosen to not stand up for Carmen, her student who identified as transgender, she would have been affirming a political stance that rejects sexualities that exist outside of the binary. If Tate forced all of her students to read from the textbook instead of seeking out *We Beat the Street,* she would have upheld a curriculum that reinforces White, male, Eurocentric ideals and perspectives. If Beverly did not require Michael to come for tutoring after the day he put his head down on his desk in class, she would have perpetuated a system in which African American males are encouraged to fail in school. Their small choices indicate their political stances, both overtly and tacitly.

When preservice candidates ask me what to say when their students ask whom they voted for in a presidential election, for instance, I tell them that their politics will likely already be known to students through the conversations they have with them and the ways in which they conduct themselves on a daily basis. If their students were to really think about it, these teachers' preference for a presidential nominee would be obvious. It is a farce to try to hide our dispositions because they infiltrate all that we do—from, as noted in Etta's case, language choices, to, as in Beverly's case, the way we respond to and frame student behavior. It may take a discerning eye to recognize, especially for teachers who may not make their commitments as explicit as Etta and Beverly do theirs, but again values undergird a person's general disposition and actions toward others. Teachers may have limitations on what they can and cannot discuss with their students in terms of their personal preferences, but NCTE's Position Statement on Academic Freedom (2014a) declares, "In academic contexts, students and teachers have the right to express their views on any matter relevant to the curriculum" (p. 1). Thus, when it comes to the matter of classroom discussions of texts and issues arise that could be considered controversial, teachers are supported in engaging in intellectual dialogue with their students. This does not preclude caution, as "Efforts to convince students to modify their beliefs or values must be academically justifiable" (p. 1). While it is therefore not the teacher's job to indoctrinate, it is hers to expose students to multiple, even opposing perspectives. NCTE's Guidelines for Dealing with Censorship (2004) insist that "the discussion of controversial topics or works does not imply endorsement or approval of the views or values suggested by those works or expressed by students in discussion of those works" (p. 3). It is okay, even welcomed, to confront controversy in the English class. If the teacher does not, who will?

## Obviating Self-Censorship

Furthermore, teachers should familiarize themselves with NCTE's position statement on "The Students' Right to Read" (2012) and the resources they have for support if a text is questioned. This will help educators feel more confident in their own choices and assuage potential self-doubt. The document, created by the body that governs standards for English teaching, affirms "The right of any individual not just to read but to read whatever he or she wants to read is basic to a democratic society" (p. 3). It also notes the difference between *selection* and *censorship,* where a teacher might choose texts for varied reasons, based on student population or reading goals, for example, but does not eliminate works on the basis of inappropriateness or controversial content.

It is the teacher's job then to honor their students' right to engage with texts but also to ensure that those works are properly considered and well chosen. Educators should remind themselves that a world without the elements that censors eliminate, such as racism and eating disorders, does not exist. To pretend otherwise "impinges upon First Amendment rights of children and adolescents and severely limits their opportunities to expand their worldviews" (Boyd & Bailey, 2009, p. 659). It falsely keeps them in an infantile state, leaving them "with an inadequate and distorted picture of the ideals, values, and problems of their culture" (NCTE, 2012, p. 4). Students deserve to know about the good, the bad, and the ugly of our world, especially if teachers expect them to become change agents. Remember too from Chapter 5 that Etta's students demonstrated a keen perceptiveness in pointing out the bawdy nature of Mercutio's jokes. The sexual content was not lost on them, and they eagerly inquired about it. Youth admit they are already well aware of issues that censors may wish to conceal, such as violence, drug use, and sex (Denzin, 2013). If educators do not use texts to bring the injustices of our world to students' attention, they will go on to accept the status quo unquestioningly, not seeing the pervasiveness of privilege and oppression in their everyday lives (Boyd & Bailey, 2009). Also, while much of the scholarship on censorship affirms parents' rights to determine what their children will read, it does not grant "the right to demand that an entire classroom, school, or district should not read a particular book or view a film" (Boyd & Bailey, 2009, p. 654). A parent requesting that his student opt out of a book, then, is a valid option and a teacher can provide an alternative.

Furthermore, teachers should be aware of the endorsement of governing bodies such as the Council for the Accreditation of Educator Preparation (CAEP), who approved social justice language in standards for the initial preparation of secondary English language arts teachers, grades 7–12 (NCTE, 2012). The National Council of Teachers of English continues its support for engaging our students with diverse perspectives in classrooms (see, for example NCTE, 2015). When key specialists in English education, members of its national organization, and accrediting institutions now agree that a social justice orientation is desirable in classroom teachers, teachers can feel less afraid to embody and act on social justice in their schools.

I cannot stress enough how having a prepared rationale for a choice to teach a work written down ahead of time and filed away can save a teacher from turmoil if she is questioned. This justification should show how the inclusion of the text has been considered from an intellectual stance and should communicate its benefit to students for any number of reasons. For instance, a teacher might assert that a text is warranted for meeting students' socioemotional needs or that it is relevant to a unit based on a time period she is teaching (Smagorinsky, 2007). Teachers should use research-based guidelines for text selection, such as those regarding multicultural literature (e.g. Louie, 2006) or queer literature (e.g. Logan, Lasswell, Hood, & Watson, 2014), and they should communicate and cite the guidelines they use. Of course, the rationale should also articulate how texts relate to the Common Core State Standards (or the standards to which the teacher's state subscribes), noting what skills the teacher is using the work to foster and outlining how she will go about achieving those goals.

Teachers should also discuss in the rationale how they "consider the contribution which each work may make to the education of the reader, its aesthetic value, its honesty, its readability for a particular group of students, and its appeal to adolescents" (NCTE, 2012, p. 3). Composing such a rationale will force the educator to ask herself why she is including a text *and* why she is excluding others. This can help avoid some subconscious self-censorship. Educators should contemplate what story they are telling, why, and what, if any, narratives they are avoiding. They can gauge their own comfort level with the texts and the issues on which they focus, and if they find themselves never feeling a sense of worry, they should think about how that might indicate that they are avoiding challenges or controversial perspectives. Perhaps most importantly, teachers must anticipate objections to the works they want to teach and include in their rationales their response to them (NCTE, 2014b). As a whole, a teacher should make good choices and defend them well.

Finally, English educators should know the policies at their school, the standard processes for challenging a text, and the supports in place to assist them in the case of a challenge. Larger schools tend to have more formalized policies for book protests (Rickman, 2010). If a teacher finds herself at an institution without a prescribed procedure in place, she should initiate one. NCTE's "Students' Right to Read" (2012) contains a "Citizen's Request for Reconsideration of a Work"(p. 6), a document that can be adapted and used for book queries. This organization suggests this document for use if a telephone conversation with a complainant is not sufficient to assuage their concern about a text. It requires the would-be censor to describe their understanding of the text, its use in the classroom, and their opposition to it. Formalizing this process safeguards against frivolous challenges and demarcates those concerns that will be investigated and validated. Teachers' familiarizing themselves with NCTE's Intellectual Freedom Center gives them a resource that can aid them personally with a challenge. The center's website (www.ncte.org/action/anti-censorship) contains a reporting form as well as resources with defenses of commonly challenged books.

If I can extend to teachers one of piece of advice related to the issue of self-censorship it is this: Be brave. The "Students' Right to Read" (2012) tells us that "the success of much censorship depends upon frightening an unprepared school or English department into some precipitous action." (p. 7). Refuse to be scared into self-censoring. The moments that have been the most rewarding in my own teaching have been those in which I have taken risks, in which I have pushed the boundaries of discussion about race and sexuality, for instance. I have admittedly been nervous about the resistance I might receive from students, concerned with specific ones in mind whose parents I know or of whose politics I am uncertain, only to find that the youth in my class were starving to talk about these topics. Taking this risk is the only way I would have known this. If teachers cannot provide students with critical but safe spaces to discuss sensitive issues, to debate in constructive classrooms, how can they expect them to know about issues and to become productive, engaged citizens? If educators don't provide them a place to wrestle with the themes most relevant in society, again I ask, who will?

These notions are merely a starting point for overcoming the obstacles encountered by social justice educators and ensuring that individual teachers are not alone in driving this work. While teaching in the classroom for social justice may begin as a sole educator's initiative and the content and pedagogies employed are her activism, the idea of social action, of moving beyond the classroom walls, should become the students' activism. Creating the conditions for students to act and guiding them in the process is the teacher's role, but it is empowered students who effect change.

# CHAPTER 7

# Conclusion

In the first chapter of this book, I posited that there are commonalities in the stories, values, and practices of teachers who enact social justice in English classrooms, hence my purpose in embarking on this journey. Etta, Beverly, and Tate are educators who seek genuine, caring relationships with their students that demonstrate their perceived value in youth. All foster their students' critical literacies, having them analyze texts for power and oppression, and all consistently seek to inspire their students toward success, regardless of students' positionalities. Yet I also recognize that each teacher has a nuanced approach and works with a specific population. Scholars such as North (2008) are quick to tell us that "Multiple pathways are necessary to create politically engaged, critically aware citizens. . . . We cannot expect a single approach to social justice education to be effective for all students in all contexts" (p. 1200). The three teachers described in this book respond specifically to what they feel their student populations need. Each has a distinct approach, which I do not wish to diminish. Thus, while I argue for the emergent, collective practices of these teachers as emblematic of social justice teaching, I also avow that successful implementation of any of those approaches must be adapted to fit the unique personality of the teacher and educational context of the students and the community.

By examining the three teachers together, I nonetheless hope to extend some instances of what it means to do social justice and how it can appear in the work of secondary English teachers. I studied these tactics of equity pedagogies related specifically to building relationships and using language strategically, analyzing how Etta purposefully engaged with students to advocate for those who are marginalized as well as how she used transformative, disruptive, and symbolic languages. I investigated Beverly's embodiment of critical caring, focusing on how she balanced an ethic of care with pushing her students toward success. From these more general approaches to students, I separated methods related to content for the explicit reason of showing that yes, there are fundamental relational and culturally responsive elements to social justice teaching—but there are precise, content-based aspects as well. These include employing texts that reflect students' subjectivities in addition to works from the canon to build students' critical literacies. Much of the current research and scholarship on social justice focuses on the pedagogical at the expense of disciplinary methods (Dyches & Boyd, 2017), instructing teachers on how to work with students from diverse backgrounds or how to honor home languages. While these are imperative, I strive to exemplify both, those related to broader cross-disciplinary approaches and those that pertain to English, as a way to maintain the importance of general classroom dynamics while introducing and asserting the centrality of content-based practices as part of social justice pedagogies.

As I elucidate through Etta, Beverly, and Tate, teachers experience some very real concerns and obstacles to social justice education. Internalizing the fear of censorship, worrying about administrative support, and being required to work within restrictive curriculum and school structures are potential barriers to equity work. Parents' reactions to controversial classroom material can prompt a teacher to avoid such material, and requirements for uniformity across teachers can stifle innovative approaches. Yet as the teachers in this book have shown, these impositions need not suppress social justice—there are support systems, such as NCTE, for teachers to draw upon in cases of censorship, and it is entirely feasible to connect curricular standards to nurturing students' critical lenses and engaging them in social action. Even beyond those avenues that Etta, Beverly, and Tate take, I argue that there are additional ways to traverse those challenges so that the goals of social justice can still be accomplished, including continued communication with parents on provocative classroom material, creating community partnerships, and allowing the students to direct civic projects. Through the examples of practicing classroom teachers and these suggestions for navigating barriers, I aim to affirm the achievability of social justice education.

Encouragement from entities such as NCTE's "The Students' Right to Read" and CAEP's standard for social justice create opportunities in schools for specifically targeted equity work and render numerous the possibilities for pedagogies and content. Etta, Beverly, and Tate are just a few examples of teachers doing social justice in their classrooms, and theirs are only some of the methods that can be employed for equity. Using them as models, teachers can expand and adapt their practices to meet their own contexts and needs. In the future, the field needs more teachers engaging in practices and with texts in ways that cultivate students' critical dispositions and engender social action.

I am hopeful for this prospective English education. I re-envision ours as a space thriving with lively conversation based on reading, dissecting, and reconstructing texts that center current events and local concerns. I imagine students engaged with social action projects, tackling issues of import to them in their immediate as well as broader contexts. I foresee the selection of new texts in classrooms, those that reflect the positions of our students and that challenge them to think and see beyond themselves. I picture students who come to value one another's differences and seek out diverse perspectives.

The realization of these possibilities relies heavily on teachers. It is up to them to create and maintain atmospheres of inquiry and criticality. It is their duty to provide occasions for their students to research the things that matter to them and to seek remedies to those issues that plague their existence. This may seem risky—how are teachers to know at first where their students will go? Such an approach involves releasing a great deal of power and enacting confidence in students, but it is worth it. When students are invested in their own learning and given responsibility, they will rise to the event. It is then the teacher's job to guide them, to determine what they need as they advance, and to design lessons accordingly. This approach does not equate to a laissez-faire one, but instead works in tandem with students toward their learning about their worlds. It places more of a demand on the teacher in terms of preparation and knowledge than, for instance, simply giving a worksheet. It requires that the teacher set up experiences for students and design the conditions for student learning behind the scenes, rather than as a leader up in front of the classroom during class time. This may be a shift from how teachers imagined their professional selves, but seeing how the students respond to this sort of teaching will serve as compensation for the efforts. My favorite lessons are those that may require a great deal of preparation on my part but that, during class, have the students focused on one another, and where my role is as an observer, questioner, and supporter.

The future of English education, beyond students engaged in equity, also involves teachers working together for justice. Schools need collaborative teacher communities that meet to plan social-justice oriented lessons and projects that bring students together across disciplinary, ability, and age-based divisions and that engage their students with their local and global communities. These teacher groups can also discuss and support one another with dilemmas of practice that are social-justice oriented, whether this be regarding fighting a school policy that oppresses a certain population of students, advocating for a student in need, or developing curriculum within the parameters of standards or mandates that simultaneously addresses social justice. As I have argued, social justice is not at odds with standards for student learning or even mandated texts. Integrating critical work may require some creativity and thoughtful planning, but it is possible. For, if Etta, Beverly, and Tate show us anything, it is that this work can—and should—be done.

# References

Albers, P., Vasquez, V. M., & Harste, J. C. (2008). A classroom with a view: Teachers, multimodality, and new literacies. *Talking Points 19*(2), 3–13.

Alexander, M. (2016). The warm demander: An equity approach. *Edutopia*. Retrieved from www.edutopia.org/blog/warm-demander-equity-approach-matt-alexander

Antrop-González, R., & Jesús, A. D. (2006). Toward a theory of critical care in urban small school reform: Examining structures and pedagogies of caring in two Latino community-based schools. *International Journal of Qualitative Studies in Education, 19*(4), 409–433.

Appleman, D. (2015). *Critical encounters in secondary English: Teaching literary theory to adolescents* (3rd ed.). New York, NY: Teachers College Press.

Asher, J. (2011). *Th1rteen r3asons why*. New York, NY: Razorbill.

Banks, J. (2010). Approaches to multicultural curriculum and reform. In J. A. Banks & C. A. McGee Banks (Eds.), *Multicultural education: Issues and perspectives* (7th ed., pp. 233–256). Hoboken, NJ: John Wiley & Sons.

Barnes, D. R. (1992). *From communication to curriculum* (2nd ed.). Portsmouth, NH: Heinemann.

Barry, B. (2005). *Why social justice matters*. Malden, MA: Polity Press.

Barton, D., & Hamilton, M. (1998). *Local literacies: Reading and writing in one community*. London, England: Routledge.

Bausell, S. B. (2017). The grammar of English education. Pedagogical possibilities of critical discourse analysis. Unpublished manuscript, School of Education, University of North Carolina at Chapel Hill, Chapel Hill, North Carolina.

Behrman, E. H. (2006). Teaching about language, power, and text: A review of classroom practices that support critical literacy. *Journal of Adolescent and Adult Literacy, 49*(6), 490–498.

Belmonte, D. (2003). *Teaching from the deep end: Succeeding with today's classroom challenges*. Thousand Oaks, CA: Corwin Press.

Bettez, S. (2011). Navigating the guilt vs. innocence dichotomy in teaching social justice. *South Atlantic Philosophy of Education Society Yearbook*, 169–181.

Boler, M. (1999). *Feeling power: Emotions and education*. London, England: Routledge.

Bomer, R. & Bomer, K. (2001). *For a better world: Reading and writing for social action*. Portsmouth, NH: Heinemann.

Boser, U. (2014). *Teacher diversity revisited.* Center for American Progress. Retrieved from www.americanprogress.org/issues/race/report/2014/05/04/88962/teacher-diversity-revisited/

Bourdieu, P. (1986). The forms of capital. In J. G. Richardson (Ed.), *Handbook of theory and research for the sociology of education* (pp. 241–258). Westport, CT: Greenwood Press.

Boyd, A., Gorham, J., Justice, J., & Anderson, J. (2013). Examining the apprenticeship of observation with preservice teachers: The practice of blogging to facilitate autobiographical reflection and critique. *Teacher Education Quarterly, 40*(3), 27–49.

Boyd, A. & Noblit, G. (2015). Engaging students in autobiographical critique as a social justice tool: Deconstructing and reconstructing narratives of meritocracy and privilege with preservice teachers. *Educational Studies 51*(6), 441–459.

Boyd, F. B. & Bailey, N. M. (2009). Censorship in three metaphors. *Journal of Adolescent & Adult Litearcy, 52*(8), 653–661.

Canadian Teachers' Federation & The Critical Thinking Consortium. (2010). *Social action projects: Making a difference K–4.* Ottawa, ON: Canadian Teachers Federation and The Critical Thinking Consortium.

Carey-Webb, A. (2001). *Literature & lives: A response-based, cultural studies approach to teaching English.* Urbana, IL: National Council of Teachers of English.

Cazden, C. B. (1986). Classroom discourse. In M. C. Wittrock (Ed.), *Handbook of research on teaching* (pp. 432–463). New York, NY: Macmillan.

Cazden, C. B. (2001). *Classroom discourse: The language of teaching and learning.* Portsmouth, NH: Heinemann.

Chouliaraki, L. (2010). Post-humanitarianism: Humanitarian communication beyond a politics of pity. *International Journal of Cultural Studies, 13,* 107–126. doi:10.1177/1367877909356720

Christensen, L. (2000). *Reading, writing, and rising up: Teaching about social justice and the power of the written word.* Milwaukee, WI: Rethinking Schools.

Cisneros, S. (1991). *The house on Mango Street.* New York, NY: Vintage Contemporaries.

Cochran-Smith, M., Barnatt, J., Lahann, R., Shakman, K., & Terrell, D. (2009). Teacher education for social justice: Critiquing the critiques. In W. Ayers, T. Quinn, & D. Stovall (Eds.), *Handbook for social justice in education* (pp. 625–639). New York, NY: Routledge.

Cochran-Smith, M., Shakman, K., Jong, C., Terrell, D. G., Barnatt, J. & McQuillan, P. (2009). Good and just teaching: The case for social justice in teacher education. *American Journal of Education, 115*(3), 347–377.

Coffey, J. (2015). Preparing to serve your people: Critical multiliteracies pedagogy in a secondary English classroom. In E. Morrell & L. Scherff (Eds.), *New directions in Teaching English* (pp. 3–16). Lanham, MD: Rowman & Littlefield.

Common Core State Standards Initiative. (2010). *English Language Arts Standards, Writing, Grade 9-10.* Retrieved from www.corestandards.org/ELA-Literacy/W/9-10/#CCSS.ELA-Literacy.W.9-10.4/

Cooper, P. M. (2003). Effective white teachers of black children: Teaching within a community. *Journal of Teacher Education, 54*(5), 413–427.

Cridland-Hughes, S. (2015). Caring critical literacy: The most radical pedagogy you can offer students. *English Journal, 105*(2), 129–132.

Curry, A. (2001). Where is Judy Blume? Controversial fiction for older children and young adults. *Journal of Youth Services in Libraries, 14*(3), 24–33.

Darder, A. (2012). *Culture and power in the classroom: Educational foundations for the schooling of bicultural students*. Boulder, CO: Paradigm Publishers.

Darragh, J. & Boyd, A. (2017). *Text selection: Perceptions of novice vs. veteran teachers*. Manuscript under review.

Davis, S., Jenkins, G., & Hunt, R., with Draper, S. M. (2005). *We beat the street: How a friendship pact led to success*. New York, NY: Puffin Books.

Delpit, L. (1995). *Other people's children: Cultural conflict in the classroom*. New York, NY: The New Press.

Delpit, L. (2008). No kinda sense. In L. Delpit & J. Kilgour Dowdy (Eds.), *The skin that we speak: Thoughts on language and culture in the classroom* (pp. 31–48). New York, NY: The New Press.

Delpit, L. (2012). *Multiplication is for white people: Raising expectations for other people's children*. New York, NY: The New Press.

Denzin, J. (2013). Boundaries for contemporary literature: The role of censorship and choice. *Journal of Adolescent & Adult Literacy, 57*(1), 7–11.

Dover, A. (2015). Teaching for social justice and the common core: Justice-oriented curriculum for language arts and literacy. *Journal of Adolescent and Adult Literacy, 59*(5), 517–527.

Downey, A. L. (2005). The transformative power of drama: Bringing literature and social justice to life. *English Journal, 95*(1), 33–39.

Duncan-Andrade, J. (2009). Note to educators: Hope required when growing roses in concrete. *Harvard Educational Review, 79*(2), 181–194.

Dyches, J. & Boyd, A. (2017). Foregrounding equity in teacher education: Toward a model of social justice pedagogical and content knowledge (SJPACK). *Journal of Teacher Education.* doi: 10.1177/0022487117705097

Ehret, C. & Hollett, T. (2014). Embodied composition in real virtualities: Adolescents' literacy practices and felt experiences moving with digital, mobile devices in school. *Research in the Teaching of English, 48*(4), 428–452.

Epstein, S. E. (2009). "[T]o carve out new orders in experience": Imagination in a social action literacy project. *English Journal, 99*(2), 61–66.

Epstein, S. E. (2014). *Teaching civic literacy projects: Student engagement with social problems*. New York, NY: Teachers College Press.

Eslinger, J. C. (2013). Caring and understanding "as nearly as possible": Towards culturally responsive caring across differences. *Critical Intersections in Education, 1*(1), 1–11.

Fairclough, N. (2010). *Critical discourse analysis* (2nd ed.). London, England: Longman.

Freedman, L. & Johnson, H. (2000/2001). Who's protecting whom?: *I Hadn't*

*Meant to Tell You This*, a case in point in confronting self-censorship in the choice of young adult literature. *Journal of Adolescent & Adult Literacy, 44*(4), 356–369.

Freire, P. (1970). *Pedagogy of the oppressed*. New York, NY: Continuum.

Frey, N. (2005). Retention, social promotion, and academic redshirting: What do we know and need to know? *Remedial and Special Education 26*(6), 332–346.

Friese, E. G., Alvermann, D. E., Parkes, A., & Rezak, A. T. (2008). Selecting texts for English Language Arts classrooms: When assessment is not enough. *English Teaching: Practice and Critique, 7*(3), 74–99.

Gallo, D. (2001). How classics create an aliterate society. *The English Journal, 90*(3), 33–39.

Gay, G. (2002). Preparing for culturally responsive teaching. *Journal of Teacher Education, 53*(2), 106–116.

Gay, G. (2010). Acting on beliefs in teacher education for cultural diversity. *Journal of Teacher Education, 61*(1–2), 143–152.

Gee, J. P. (1996). *Social linguistics and literacies: Ideology in discourses* (2nd ed.). London, England: Taylor and Francis.

Gee, J. (2015). *Social linguistics and literacies: Ideology in discourses* (5th ed.). New York, NY: RoutledgeFalmer.

George, T. (Producer & Director). (2005). *Hotel Rwanda* [Motion picture]. United States: MGM.

Georing, C. Z., & Connors, S. P. (2014). Exemplars and epitaphs: Defending young adult literature. *Talking Points, 25*(2), 15–21.

Glazier, J., & Seo, J.A. (2005). Multicultural literature and discussion as mirror and window? *Journal of Adolescent and Adult Literacy, 48*(8), 686–700.

Golden, J. (2008). A conversation with Linda Christensen on social justice education. *English Journal, 97*(6), 59–64.

Grant, C. A., & Agosto, V. (2008). Teacher capacity and social justice in teacher education. In M. Cochran-Smith, S. Feiman-Nemser, K. E. Demers, & J. McIntyre (Eds.), *Handbook of Research on Teacher Education: Enduring Questions and Changing Contexts* (pp. 175–200). New York, NY: Routledge.

Green, J. (2005). *Looking for Alaska*. New York, NY: Speak.

Gurdon, M. C. (2011, June 4). Darkness too visible. *The Wall Street Journal*. Retrieved from online.wsj.com/news/articles/SB10001424052702303657404576 357622592697038

Hall, S. (1997). *Representation and the media*. Media Education Foundation Transcript. Retrieved from www.mediaed.org/assets/products/409/transcript_409. pdf

Hansberry, L. (1959). *A raisin in the sun*. New York, NY: Random House.

Heath, S. B. (1983). *Ways with words: Language, life, and work in communities and classrooms*. Cambridge, MA: Cambridge University Press.

Henry, G. T., Purtell, K. M., Bastian, K. C., Fortner, C. K., Thompson, C. L., Campbell, S. L., and Patterson, K. M. (2014). The effects of teacher entry portals on student achievement. *Journal of Teacher Education, 65*, 7–23.

Hess, D. E. (2009). *Controversy in the classroom: The democratic power of discussion.* New York, NY: Routledge.

Hinchey, P. H. (2004). *Becoming a critical educator: Defining a classroom identity, designing a critical pedagogy.* New York, NY: Peter Lang.

Hines, M. B., & Johnson, J. (2007). Teachers and students as agents of change: Toward a taxonomy of the literacies of social justice. In D. Row, R. Jimenez, D. Compton, D. Dickinson, Y. Kim, K. Leander, & V. Risko (Eds.), *2007 Yearbook of the National Reading Conference* (pp. 281–292). Oak Creek, WI: National Reading Conference

Hosseini, K. (2003). *The kite runner.* New York, NY: The Berkley Publishing Group.

Hosseini, K. (2008). *A thousand splendid suns.* London, England: Bloomsbury.

Hull, G. A., & Nelson, M. E. (2005). Locating the semiotic power of multimodality. *Written Communication, 22*(2), 224–261.

Hurston, Z. N. (1994). *Their eyes were watching God.* New York, NY: Harper Perennial Modern Classics. (Original work published in 1937.)

Hytten, K., & Warren, J. (2003). Engaging whiteness: How racial power gets reified in education. *Qualitative Studies in Education, 16*(1), 65–89.

Janks, H., Dixon, K., Ferreira, A., Granville, S., & Newfield, D. (2013). *Doing critical literacy: Texts and activities for students and teachers.* New York, NY: Routledge.

Jewitt, C. (2008). Multimodality and literacy in school classrooms. *Review of Research in Education, 32,* 241–267.

Johnson, J. (2012). "A rainforest in front of a bulldozer": The literacy practices of teacher candidates committed to social justice. *English Education, 44*(2), 147–179.

Kalantzis, M. & Cope, B. (2000). A multiliteracies pedagogy: A pedagogical supplement. In B. Cope and M. Kalantzis (Eds.), *Multiliteracies: Literacy learning and the design of social futures* (pp. 237–246). New York, NY: Routledge.

Kincheloe, J. L. (2008). *Critical pedagogy primer.* New York, NY: Peter Lang.

King, Martin Luther, Jr. (1963, August). *I have a dream.* Speech presented at the March on Washington. Washington, DC.

Kirkland, D., with Filipiak, D. (2008). Quiet tensions in meaning: A conversation with a "social justice" teacher. In s. j. miller, L. B. Beliveau, T. DeStigter, D. Kirkland, & P. Rice (Eds.), *Narratives of social justice teaching: How English teachers negotiate theory and practice between preservice and inservice spaces* (pp. 45–64). New York, NY: Peter Lang.

Kress, G., & van Leeuwen, T. (2001). *Multimodal discourse: The modes and media of contemporary communication.* London, UK: Edward Arnold.

Kumashiro, K. (2004). *Against common sense: Teaching and learning toward social justice* (Rev. ed.). New York, NY: Routledge.

Ladson-Billings, G. (1995). Toward a theory of culturally relevant pedagogy. *American Educational Research Journal, 32,* 465–491.

Ladson-Billings, G. (2006). "Yes, but how do we do it": Practicing culturally relevant pedagogy. In J. Landsman & C. Lewis (Eds.), *White teachers/diverse classrooms: A guide to building inclusive schools, promoting high expectations, and eliminating racism* (pp. 29–41). Herndon, VA: Stylus Publishing.

Landt, S. M. (2006). Multicultural literature and young adolescents: A kaleidoscope of opportunity. *Journal of Adolescent & Adult Literacy, 49*(8), 690–697.

Lent, R. (2016, September 25). Censorship by committee [Web log post]. Retrieved from blogs.ncte.org/index.php/2016/09/censorship-by-committee/

Logan, S. R., Lasswell, T. A., Hood, Y., & Watson, D. C. (2014). Criteria for the selection of young adult queer literature. *English Journal, 103*(5), 30–41.

Lortie, D. (1975). *Schoolteacher: A sociological study*. Chicago: University of Chicago Press.

Louie, B. Y. (2006). Guiding principles for teaching multicultural literature. *Reading Teacher, 59*(5), 438–448.

Luke, A. (2000). Critical literacy in Australia: A matter of context and standpoint. *Journal of Adolescent and Adult Literacy, 43*(5), 448–461.

Macklemore & Lewis, R. (2012). A wake. On *The Heist* [CD]. Seattle, WA: Macklemore LLC-ADA.

Mancina, H. (2005). Empowering students through a social-action writing project. *English Journal, 94*(6), 31–35.

Matias, C. E., & Zembylas, M. (2014). "When saying you care is not really caring": Emotions of disgust, whiteness ideology, and teacher education. *Critical Studies in Education, 55*(3), 319–337. doi: 10.1080/17508487.2014.922489

McCarthy-Miller, B., & Mitchell, J. (Directors), & Hach, H. (Writer). (2007). *Legally blonde: The musical* [Motion picture]. United States: MTV.

McIntosh, P. (1989). White privilege: Unpacking the invisible knapsack. *Peace and Freedom Magazine*, 10–12. Retrieved from www.deanza.edu/faculty/lewisjulie/White%20Priviledge%20Unpacking%20the%20Invisible%20Knapsack.pdf

McLaren, P. (2003). *Life in schools: An introduction to critical pedagogy in the foundations of education* (4th ed.). Boston, MA: Pearson Education.

Mendez, J. (2014). Revisiting "sordid fantasies": Using detournement as an approach to qualitative inquiry. In J. Trier (Ed.), *Detournement as pedagogical praxis* (pp. 195–209). Rotterdam, The Netherlands: Sense Publishers

miller, s. j. (2014). Cultivating a disposition for sociospatial justice in English teacher education. *Teacher Education and Practice, 27*(1), 44–74.

Moje, E. B., & Hinchman, K. (2004). Culturally responsive practices for youth literacy learning. In J. Dole, & T. Jetton (Eds.), *Adolescent literacy research and practice* (pp. 331–350). New York, NY: Guilford Press.

Monroe, B. (2002). *Teaching critical engagement*. Retrieved from public.wsu.edu/~bjmonroe/323teachingCE.pdf

Morrell, E., & Duncan-Andrade, J. (2005/2006). Popular culture and critical media pedagogy in secondary literacy classrooms. *International Journal of Learning, 12*, 1–11.

Moss, B. (2013). The Common Core Text Exemplars—A Worthy New Canon or Not? *Voices from the Middle, 21*(1), 48–52.

Murray, D. (2014). The making of a perfect speech. *Ragan's PR Daily*. Retrieved from

www.prdaily.com/Main/Articles/The_making_of_a_perfect_speech_15941.
aspx

Myers, W. D. (1999). *Monster*. New York, NY: HarperCollins.

Nadal, K. L. (2008). Preventing racial, ethnic, gender, sexual minority, disability, and religious microaggressions: Recommendations for promoting positive mental health. *Prevention in Counseling Psychology: Theory, Research, Practice and Training, 2*(1), 22–27.

National Council for Teachers of English & The International Reading Association. (2012). *Standards for the English language arts*. Retrieved from www.ncte.org/standards/ncte-ira

National Council of Teachers of English. (2004). *Guidelines for Dealing with Censorship of Nonprint and Multimedia Materials*. Retrived from www.ncte.org/positions/statements/censorshipofnonprint

National Council of Teachers of English. (2012). *The students' right to read*. Retrieved from www.ncte.org/positions/statements/righttoreadguideline

National Council of Teachers of English. (2014a). *NCTE Position Statement on Academic Freedom*. Retrieved from www.ncte.org/positions/statements/academic-freedom

National Council of Teachers of English. (2014b). *Censorship Now: Revisiting* The Students' Right to Read (Policy research brief). Urbana, IL: Author.

National Council of Teachers of English. (2015). *Resolution on the Need for Diverse Children's and Young Adult Books*. Retrieved from www.ncte.org/positions/statements/diverse-books

Nelson, K. (2013). *Nelson Mandela*. New York, NY: Katherine Tegen Books/HarperCollins.

New London Group. (1996). A pedagogy of multiliteracies: Designing social futures. *Harvard Educational Review, 66*(1), 60–92.

Noddings, N. (2005). *The challenge to care in schools* (2nd ed.). New York, NY: Teachers College Press.

North, C. (2008). What is all this talk about social justice? Mapping the terrain of education's latest catchphrase. *Teachers College Record, 110*, 1182–1206.

Parsons, E. C. (2006). From caring as a relation to culturally relevant caring: A white teacher's bridge to black students. *Equity and Excellence in Education 38*(1), 25–34.

Patterson, J. A., Gordon, J. & Groves Price, P. (2008). The color of caring: Race and the implementation of educational reform. *The Journal of Educational Foundations, 22* (3/4), 97–116.

Peterson, B. (2007). Teaching for social justice: One teacher's journey. In W. Au, B. Bigelow, & S. Karp (Eds.), *Rethinking our classrooms: Teaching for equity and justice* (New ed., pp. 28–35). Milwaukee, WI: Rethinking Schools, Ltd.

Rap Genius. (2014). *Macklemore and Ryan Lewis lyrics*. Retrieved from rapgenius.com/Macklemore-and-ryan-lewis-a-wake-lyrics

Rickman, W. (2010). A study of self-censorship by school librarians. *School Library Research, 13*, 1–21.

Rostand, E. (1985). *Cyrano de Bergerac* (A. Burgess, Trans.). New York, NY: Applause. (Original work published in 1897.)

Rymes, B. (2015). *Classroom discourse analysis: Tools for critical reflection* (2nd ed.). New York, NY: Routledge.

Sanders, J., & Albers, P. (2010). Multimodal literacies: An introduction. In J. Sanders & P. Albers (Eds.), *Literacies, the arts, and multimodality* (pp. 1–25). Urbana, IL: National Council of Teachers of English.

Satrapi, M. (2004). *Persepolis* (M. Ripa, Trans.). New York, NY: Pantheon. (Original work published in 2000.)

Schieble, M. (2012). Critical conversations on whiteness with young adult literature. *Journal of Adolescent & Adult Literacy, 56*(3), 212–221.

Schieble, M. (2014). Reframing equity under Common Core: A commentary on the text exemplar list for Grades 9–12. *English Teaching: Practice and Critique, 13*(1).

Segall, A. (2004). Revisiting pedagogical content knowledge: The pedagogy of content/the content of pedagogy. *Teaching and Teacher Education, 20,* 489–504. doi: 10.1016/j.tate.2004.04.006

Sensoy, Ö., & DiAngelo, R. (2012). *Is everyone really equal? An introduction to key concepts in social justice education.* New York, NY: Teachers College Press.

Shevalier, R., & McKenzie, B. A. (2012). Culturally responsive teaching as an ethics-and-care-based approach to urban education. *Urban Education, 47*(6), 1086–1105.

Smagorinsky, P. (2007). *Teaching English by design: How to create and carry out instructional units.* Portsmouth, NH: Heinemann.

Stallworth, B.J., Gibbons, L., & Fauber, L. (2006). It's not on the list: An exploration of teachers' perspectives on using multicultural literature. *Journal of Adolescent & Adult Literacy, 49*(6), 478–489.

"Standards in your state." (2016). Common Core State Standards Initiative. Retrieved February 15, 2016, from www.corestandards.org/standards-in-your-state/

Street, B. V. (2003). What's "new" in new literacy studies? Critical approaches to literacy in theory and practice. *Current Issues in Comparative Education, 5*(2) 77–91.

Tannen, D. (2007). *Talking voices: Repetition, dialogue, and imagery in conversational Discourse* (2nd ed.). Cambridge, England: Cambridge University Press.

Thompson, D. M., & Singh, A. (Producers) & Chadwick, J. (Director). (2013). *Mandela: Long walk to freedom* [Motion picture]. United States: Videovision.

Tucker, B. (2012). The flipped classroom: Online instruction at home frees class time for learning. *EducationNext, 12*(1). Retrieved from educationnext.org/the-flipped-classroom/

Urrieta, L., Jr. (2010). *Working from within: Chicana and Chicano activist educators in whitestream schools.* Tucson, AZ: University of Arizona Press.

Vasquez, J. A. (1988). Contexts of learning for minority students. *Educational Forum, 56,* 6–11.

Vasudevan, L., & Kerr, K. R. (2016). "Unflattening" our ways of seeing, reading, and writing. *Journal of Adolescent & Adult Literacy, 60*(1), 103–105.

Vasudevan, L., Rodriquez, K., Hibbert, M., Fernandez, E., & Park, A. (2014). Cosmopolitan literacies of belonging in an after-school program with court-involved youths. *Journal of Adolescent & Adult Literacy, 57*(7), 538–548.

Walker, A. (1982). *The color purple.* Boston, MA: Mariner.

Walker, M. (2003, June). Framing social justice in education: What does the "capabilities" approach offer? *British Journal of Educational Studies, 51*(2), 168–187.

Wallowitz, L. (2008). Introduction: Critical literacies defined. In L. Wallowitz (Ed.), *Critical literacy as resistance: Teaching for social justice across the secondary curriculum* (pp. 1–9). New York, NY: Peter Lang Publishing, Inc.

Watkins, N., & Ostenson, J. (2015). Navigating the text selection gauntlet: Exploring factors that influence English teachers' choices. *English Education, 47*(3), 245–275.

Wiesel, E. (1960). *Night.* (S. Rodway, Trans.). New York, NY: Hill & Wang. (Original work published in 1955.)

Yoon, B., Simpson, A., & Haag, C. (2010). Assimilation ideology: Critically examining underlying messages in multicultural literature. *Journal of Adolescent & Adult Literacy, 54*(2), 109–118.

Young, S. L. B. (2009). Breaking the silence: Critical literacy and social action. *English Journal, 98*(4), 109–115.

Zeichner, K. M. (2009). *Teacher education and the struggle for social justice.* New York, NY: Routledge.

Zusak, M. (2005). *The book thief.* New York, NY: Random House.

# Index

Occupation Project, 68–69
persuasive speeches unit, 71–72
and Professional Learning
  Community, 73–74
resource constraints, 73–74, 109
social justice content, 81, 87–88
social justice story, 27–31
standards and social justice, 65,
  69–72
teaching to the test, 70–71
text selection, 65–74, 75, 81, 87–89
time constraints, 109

Wordle, 50

Yoon, B., 113
Young, S. L. B., 96–97, 98, 101–102
Yousafzai, Malala, 82

Zeichner, K. M., 105
Zembylas, M., 10, 53–54
Zusak, Marcus, 76

# About the Author

*Ashley S. Boyd* is assistant professor of English education at Washington State University where she teaches graduate courses on critical and cultural theory and undergraduate courses on English methods and young adult literature. A former secondary English language arts teacher, Ashley's current scholarship examines practicing teachers' social justice pedagogies and their critical content knowledge, explores how young adult literature is an avenue for cultivating students' critical literacies, and investigates the implementation of state-mandated tribal curriculum in secondary schools in Washington. Ashley loves working with preservice teachers, spending time with her friends and family, and traveling to warm places. She has recently published in the *Journal of Teacher Education*, *Educational Studies*, the *International Journal of Critical Pedagogy*, and the *ALAN Review*.